Lebanese Women
at the Crossroads

Lebanese Women at the Crossroads

Caught between Sect and Nation

Nelia Hyndman-Rizk

LEXINGTON BOOKS

Lanham • Boulder • New York • London

Published by Lexington Books
An imprint of The Rowman & Littlefield Publishing Group, Inc.
4501 Forbes Boulevard, Suite 200, Lanham, Maryland 20706
www.rowman.com

6 Tinworth Street, London SE11 5AL, United Kingdom

British Library Cataloguing in Publication Information Available

Library of Congress Cataloging-in-Publication Data Available

ISBN 978-1-4985-2274-8 (cloth)
ISBN 978-1-4985-2275-5 (electronic)

I dedicate this study to all those who have searched for an answer to the women's rights puzzle in Lebanon and the activists who work hard every day to make a difference.

Contents

List of Map, Figures, and Tables

MAP

FIGURES

TABLES

List of Abbreviations

ABAAD	Resource Centre for Gender Equality
AiW	Arab Institute for Women—formerly the Institute for Women's Studies in the Arab World (IWSAW)
BAHITHAT	The Lebanese Association of Women Researchers or LAWR
BLOG	Weblog, Online diary
CEDAW	Convention on the Elimination of All Forms of Discrimination against Women
CFUWI	Committee for the Follow-up on Women's Issues
CRTD.A	Collective for Research and Training on Development-Action
EU	European Union
FBD	Father's Brother's Daughter: a form of marriage between a son and his paternal first cousin
GDI	Gender Development Index
GDP	Gross Domestic Product
IPU	Inter Parliamentary Union
ISIS	Islamic State of Iraq and Syria
KAFA	Enough Violence and Exploitation
LCW	Lebanese Council of Women
LF	Lebanese Forces
LNM	Lebanese National Movement
MENA	Middle East and North Africa
NCLW	National Commission for Lebanese Women
NGO	Non-governmental organization
NIMBY	Not in my neighborhood
SMT	Social movement theory

UN WOMEN	United Nations Women's entity dedicated to gender equality and the empowerment of women
UNDP	United Nations Development Program
UNFPA	United Nations Population Fund
UNICEF	United Nations Children Fund
UNIFEM	United Nations Development Fund for Women
WF	Women in Front
WRO	Women's Rights Organization
WUNC	Worthiness, unity in numbers, and commitment

Acknowledgments

I wish to thank all participants in this study who gave their time and insights, as well as the research assistants who worked on the study, Sibel Attasayi and Sara Al Mokdad, for their time and dedication. I thank the University of New South Wales (UNSW), Canberra, for supporting this research, with a Faculty Special Research Grant and travel assistance. I also thank Lexington Middle East Studies, which has supported the project over the years. I also thank the Lebanese Emigration Research Centre and the Arab Institute for Women (AiW) for their support and the Tampere Peace Research Institute (Tapri), at the University of Tampere, for supporting my writing as a visiting scholar. Last but not least, I thank my family for their support and interest in my research.

Preface

A Social and Political Transformation is Taking Place in Lebanon

Thirty years after the end of the Lebanese Civil War, a process of transformation is under way in Lebanon. In the October Revolution, which started on October 17, 2019, the Lebanese people occupied Riad Al Solh Square in the capital, Beirut, as well as the streets of smaller towns and cities throughout the country. The popular call, "the people demand the fall of the regime," echoed the catch cry of the Arab Spring of 2011.[1] According to street protestors, "all of them means all," the entire government should resign, all ministers, from all confessions. They called for an end to Lebanon's sectarian political system,[2] and a technocratic government to guide the transition to secular government, which would constitute a major change for the Lebanese polity. Prime Minister Hariri finally capitulated and resigned[3] on Tuesday October 29 at 4 p.m., sending the entire government into caretaker mode. Yet, the process of transformation taking place is as much a social revolution as it is a political one, because the Lebanese people are asserting a national and civic identity over a sectarian one.

Like other protest movements sweeping the world in late 2019, from Chile to Iraq,[4] economic crisis, inequality, and government corruption were the three key drivers of Lebanon's leaderless protest movement. The spark was a proposed US 20c tax on the popular social media application WhatsApp, which bypasses phone services in a country with high prices for telecommunications.[5] However, the near-collapse of the economy[6] from record high debt, running at 150 percent of the GDP, high youth unemployment, unaffordable medical costs, and rampant corruption[7] contributed to public discontent. Protestors decided that life couldn't get any worse without a government than with a dysfunctional one.

The latest uprising represents a significant watershed for Lebanon, as it crossed the sectarian divide[8] and closed roads, schools, and banks for more than two weeks. It was led by youth and civil society activists, many of whom were born[9] after Lebanon's civil war of 1975–1990. The uprising built on Lebanon's garbage crisis movement of 2015, discussed in chapter 5 of this book. Women were in the front row,[10,11,12] blocking roads, forming a human buffer between security forces and protestors, and joining a human chain[13] from the north to the south of the country. Even the diaspora[14] played a part, organizing solidarity marches and gatherings from New York to Sydney.[15]

Lebanon has an opportunity to move forward from the legacies of colonialism and the post-civil war order, to form a secular, pluralistic democracy, based on civil rights, women's rights, and public accountability. However, there are many challenges to be resolved first, least of which is a new electoral law, without sectarian quotas, the reform of Lebanon's plural personal status codes, and extending nationality rights to women, as discussed in chapters 3 to 6 of this book. There will be winners and losers in this political and social transformation but resolving the gender equality deficit will be a critical first step.

WHY GENDER EQUALITY IS IMPORTANT IN LEBANON

I began researching this book seven years ago, on a field trip to Lebanon in 2012. I arrived interested in how gender relations in Lebanon were changing in the Arab Spring. Driving down the main highway between Beirut and Tripoli, I noticed a billboard advertising civil marriage packages to Cyprus, with a picture of a happy couple. I wondered what was different about civil marriage to other forms of marriages in Lebanon and why couples go overseas. I found myself in the middle of a national debate on changing gender roles, the quest for gender equality, and the changing nature of the marriage contract in contemporary Lebanon. Return trips in 2013 and 2016 further consolidated the research findings and resulted in the viewpoints and arguments presented in this book.

The research findings identified four intersecting issues regarding the changing political, social, and gender dynamics in Lebanon, which set the context for this study and the October Revolution of 2019. First, the development of transnational interaction between Lebanon and the diaspora communities around the world, including the Gulf States, has led to the internationalization of Lebanese society. Today Lebanon has a population which is highly mobile, is multilingual, and travels frequently between international hubs. In addition to internationalization, Lebanon has undergone a process of urbanization, with most of the population no longer residing in villages in the countryside, participating in agriculture as their primary occupation. Today

88 percent of the population, of approximately 6 million people, reside in urban areas.[16]

Second, while Lebanon has a high level of human development, according to the UNDP (2019), with a score of .757 on Human Development Index, it lags behind in the Gender Development Index (GDI), with a score of .889, placing it in the fifth group of countries with a large gap between males and females. Consequently, it has high levels of gender inequality, a problem shared across the region, referred to as the Middle East and North Africa (MENA) Puzzle (World Bank 2013). Despite a steady increase in the rate of female educational attainment, which is among the highest in the Arab World, with a literacy rate of 89 percent, overall, and 85 percent for women across all age groups (UNESCO 2019), the female labor force participation remains stubbornly low, with only 23 percent of Lebanese women active in the labor force (UNDP 2019). Moreover, the proportion of female enrolments in secondary education has expanded and reached 63 percent in 2017, while the proportion of female enrolments in tertiary education was 46 percent in 2014, exceeding the male rate of 39 percent.[17] In all, young women have achieved high rates of educational attainment in Lebanon today, even in comparison to their mothers and grandmothers, as the literacy rate for women in the over-sixty-five age group remains 46 percent (UNESCO 2019). Moreover, the expansion in educational opportunity has contributed to a change in attitudes and expectations regarding career, marriage, and family among young women, which remain largely unmet by the current gender status quo.

Third, while no formal census has been conducted since 1932, during the French Mandate, the relative balance between Lebanon's religious sects is thought to have changed, in part due to emigration over the course of a century, especially during the civil war, when Christian emigration outstripped Muslim emigration. Consequently, Christians no longer constitute a majority of Lebanon's population, as they did at the time of the National Pact of 1943. Rather, it is estimated that Christians (Orthodox and Catholics) now comprise some 37 percent of the voting population and Muslims (Sunni, Shi'ite, and Druze) approximately 60 percent (Economist 2016). The change in the balance between the religious sects has led to a corresponding adjustment to the "magic formula," which apportions seats in parliament between the religious sects. The Ta'if Agreement, which ended the civil war in 1989, established parity between Christians and Muslims in parliament. Yet problems persist, with frequent political deadlocks and a lack of public accountability, leading street protestors to call for an end to confessionalism and a shift to a secular system of government. The outcome of the October Revolution will determine the future of Lebanon's confessional political system, which chapter 2 of this book examines more closely.

Finally, balancing sectarian representation in parliament is not the only problem of representation the country faces, as Lebanon has one of the lowest representations of women in parliament in the world. It ranked 183rd out of 193 countries in 2019, according to the Inter Parliamentary Union (IPU 2019), a point chapter 5 of this book examines further. In short, the sectarian quota trumps a women's quota. Yet, without sufficient women in parliament, it is difficult to pass progressive legislation, which can improve gender quality. What is more, when I interviewed women's rights activists, academics, lawyers, and policy makers on the key challenges facing Lebanese women today, the problems and complexities which derive from Lebanon's plural personal status code system, whereby family law is located within religious law, were cited as the enduring impediment to gender equality in Lebanon. Lebanon has fifteen personal status codes for eighteen recognized religious communities, comprising both Christians and Muslims. While the secularization of Lebanon's political and legal system was frequently identified as the solution to Lebanon's confessional contradictions and gender equality deficit, by activists, this study examines the link between the introduction of civil marriage and women's rights and whether the introduction of the former would guarantee the latter. Furthermore, if the gender equality deficit is only attributed to religious law, then why do Lebanese citizenship laws also discriminate against women, by precluding them from passing their nationality to their children?

The findings presented in this book are based on face-to-face interviews, two online surveys, and historical and ethnographic research conducted over a seven-year period to understand the origins of Lebanon's system of legal pluralism, the consociational division of power, and the gender equality deficit. While the links between Lebanon's confessional power sharing system, colonialism, and class have been well examined in the literature, a gap is evident in the literature on the role of gender in both reproducing and transforming the confessional political system in Lebanon. If the division between religious and civil law has been central to gender inequality in Lebanon, due to differential citizenship and marriage rights, this book asks the central question, *is secular citizenship the key to resolving the women's rights puzzle?*

The chapters that follow explore how women's rights activists seek to transform Lebanese society, politically and socially, to bring about civil rights and women's rights, by considering the following: online/offline activism, the campaign for a domestic violence law, the women's nationality campaign, the women's quota in parliament, intersectional campaigns, such as the #YouStink movement, and the campaign for civil marriage reform. On balance, this book finds that women are caught between sect and nation in Lebanon, due to the dual legal system and relational citizenship rights. However, a secularization process is underway in Lebanon, as the October Revolution highlights; while it is not a panacea, it can provide an alternative to religious family laws and political sectarianism by harmonizing personal status laws and improving gender equality. Furthermore, interreligious civil marriage has the potential to change the mode of self-identification in Lebanon from sect to nation. While the Arab Spring political revolutions remain ongoing and unfinished, the case of Lebanon highlights the importance of an accompanying gender revolution, which links civil rights and women's rights, because gender equality strengthens the democratization process.

Nelia Hyndman-Rizk
Canberra, Australia
November 2019

NOTES

1. See Emily Lewis and Ghada Alsharif, Daily Star: https://www.dailystar.com.lb/News/Lebanon-News/2019/Oct-29/494506-protests-show-no-sign-of-letting-up-despite-rain-fatigue.ashx.

2. See Mersiha Gadzo, Al Jazeera: https://www.aljazeera.com/news/2019/10/lebanon-protests-difficult-delicate-situation-hezbollah-191027053143258.html.

3. See Daily Star, http://www.dailystar.com.lb/News/Lebanon-News/2019/Oct-30/494593-hariri-bows-to-the-peoples-will.ashx.

4. See Zena Chamas, ABC News: https://www.abc.net.au/news/2019-10-29/protests-around-the-world-explained/11645682.

5. See Eamon Kircher-Allen, Daily Star, http://www.dailystar.com.lb/News/Lebanon-News/2008/Aug-13/54278-sky-high-cell-phone-service-prices-have-no-easy-answer.ashx.

6. See Daily Star: http://www.dailystar.com.lb/Business/Local/2019/Oct-28/494469-lebanons-central-bank-gov-says-country-is-days-away-from-economic-collapse.ashx?utm_source=Magnet%26utm_medium=Related%20Articles%20widget%26utm_campaign=Magnet%20tools.

7. Lebanon was ranked 138th out of 180 countries by Transparency International, https://www.transparency.org/country/LBN.

8. See Lina Khatib, Al Jazeera: https://www.aljazeera.com/indepth/opinion/lebanon-experiencing-social-revolution-191020065959490.html.

9. See Bruno Lefort, Politiikasta: https://politiikasta.fi/some-keys-to-understand-the-popular-uprising-in-lebanon/.

10. See Nicholas Frakes, Al Monitor: https://www.al-monitor.com/pulse/originals/2019/10/women-stand-strong-on-the-frontlines-of-lebanons-protests.html.

11. See Al Araby: https://www.alaraby.co.uk/english/indepth/2019/10/22/revolutionaries-not-babes-stop-objectifying-lebanons-women-protesters.

12. See Rubina Abu Zeinab-Chahine, The Daily Star: https://www.dailystar.com .lb/News/Lebanon-News/2019/Nov-06/495063-lebanese-women-ahead-of-the-c urve-in-protests-too.ashx.

13. See the Guardian: https://www.theguardian.com/world/2019/oct/27/lebanon-p rotesters-form-human-chain-across-entire-country.

14. See Jad Baghdadi in The Daily Star: http://www.dailystar.com.lb/News/ Lebanon-News/2019/Oct-28/494427-near-and-far-diaspora-keeps-up-support-for-pr otesters.ashx?utm_source=Magnet%26utm_medium=Related%20Articles%20widg et%26utm_campaign=Magnet%20tools.

15. See Libanus IV, The 961: https://www.the961.com/diaspora/sydney-solida rity-protest-for-lebanon-expects-massive-participation.

16. Lebanon also has a substantial population of Palestinian and Syrian refugees, thought to number more than 1 million. See http://worldpopulationreview.com/co untries/lebanon-population/.

17. World Bank, School Enrolment, Tertiary, female https://data.worldbank.org/ indicator/SE.TER.CUAT.MS.FE.ZS?locations=LB. See also http://uis.unesco.org/ country/LB.

LEBANON

Aarida
Al Qubayyat
Halba

Tripoli Hmaïra
LIBAN-NORD Al Hirmil

Chekka Déddé Ehdèn Qaa
Amyun Amioûn Bcharre
Batroûn El Hrâyeq
Rashana Al Labwa Aarsâl
Al Hrazmin El Aarich
Biblos Chlifa Maqnah

Mediterranean Ad Dahr Quartaba
sea
MONT-LIBAN Beit **BEQAA**
Biskinta Shama Braytal
BEYROUTH Bikfraya
Beirut Riyaq
Baabda
Ash Shuwayfat **Zahlah**
Alayh
Dâmoûr Hansh
Baaqline Mousa
Al Bashiqiyah Kamid
Aïn Zebdé al Lawz

Al 'Aqabah
Sidon Al Qir'awn **SYRIA**
Qarasoun
Dahr
al Ahmar
Al Insariyah Habbush 'Aramtah

NABATIYE
Tyre **Nabatiye** Bani
Hayyan
LIBAN-SUD
Chakra
Ramyah Aïtaroun

Golan Heights
(Israel occupied) UNDOF
Zone

ISRAEL

Map 1   Map of Lebanon. *Source*: www.mapsopensource.com.

Part I

FORMATIONS

The first part of this book examines the formation of the Lebanese consociational system of government and law and the implications for women's rights. Chapter 2 provides a short history of Lebanon, as an historic refuge for minorities in the Ottoman Empire to the postcolonial period, and considers three key characteristics of Lebanese history: a sizeable Christian population, a long exposure to the West, and the impact of Lebanon's confessional power-sharing system on gender relations. Chapter 3 examines the formation of Lebanon's family law system, based on plural personal status codes, their relationship to the *millet* system, under the Ottoman Empire, and the continuity between the ancient laws of the Middle East and today. Women's separate and unequal status is considered in each of Lebanon's fifteen recognized personal status codes, comprising Muslim and Christian family law.

Chapter 1

Introduction

This study builds on recent scholarship on gendered citizenship in the Arab World, in the context of the Arab Spring. It examines how discourses of secularism and equal civil rights have informed the contemporary Lebanese women's movement in their campaigns for a domestic violence law in 2014, women's nationality rights, a women's quota in parliament, the reform of personal status law, and the recognition of civil marriage in 2013. The study argues that women are caught between sect and nation in Lebanon, due to Lebanon's system of legal pluralism, which makes a division between religious and civil law. While both jurisdictions allocate women relational rights, guided by the logic of patrilineal descent, women's inequality is central to the reproduction of sectarian difference and patriarchal control, respectively, within the confessional political system as a whole. Thus, in order for political change to occur, a social and legal revolution is a necessary first step. Hence, a dual struggle is necessary (Khamis and Mili 2017), the first for equal political and civil rights, and the second for equal legal rights, in relation to personal status law. Let us start with the turmoil across the Middle East since 2011, following a series of uprisings that started in Tunisia, which set the context for this study.

THE ARAB SPRING

The Middle Eastern region has seen the rise and fall of the so-called Arab Spring (Dabashi 2012, 7), a term used to describe the upsurge in citizens' rights campaigns for democratization across the Middle East in the aftermath of revolutions in Tunisia on January 14, 2011, and Egypt on February 11, 2011, as well as ongoing revolutions, counterrevolutions, and democratic transitions in a number of other Arab states, including Syria and Lebanon (Korotayev et al. 2014). For Dabashi (2012, 7–8), the Arab Spring optimistically signaled an end to postcolonialism and the exhaustion of the three key postcolonial philosophies: nationalism, socialism, and Islamism in search of freedom, social justice, and dignity. Elizabeth Thompson (2013), alternately, theorized that the Arab Spring was not entirely new but represented an unfinished struggle for constitutional government in the region, which started in the mid-nineteenth century. Despite differing interpretations of the origins, purpose, and outcome of the Arab Spring, it is apparent that the process of democratic transition that emerged in 2011 has been nonlinear and open ended, with variable success across the region.

A democratic tsunami has not occurred in the Arab World, in Szmolka's (2015, 73–95) final analysis, but rather, a fifth wave of political change with variable results ranging from democratization, liberalization, to new forms of authoritarianism and cosmetic reforms. After the early optimism of the Arab Spring, the process of democratic transition appears to have stalled (Ahmed and Macharia 2013). The new social movements have been divided between secular and religious social forces and, subsequently, the first elected parliaments after the revolutions in Tunisia and Egypt saw strong election results for Islamist-based political parties (Noueihed and Warren 2012). Furthermore, both Tunisia and Egypt experienced political crises between the elected Islamist-dominated parliaments and secularist opposition parties and women's rights activists. Subsequently, the Morsi-led Muslim Brotherhood government was overthrown by the Egyptian military in July 2013.

While Tunisia eventually saw a compromise between Islamist and secular social forces and a new constitution on January 26, 2014, which enshrined gender equality (Mili 2017, 48), for Szmolka (2015), the transition model determined the success or failure of the Arab Spring, in different contexts, and distinguished between exclusionary, nonconsensual, and inclusive consensual transitions. In the former case, Egypt, nonaccountable actors determined the result of the transition, whereas in the latter case, Tunisia, agreements between political actors, both secular and Islamist, and concessions by the predominant party brought about a successful transition. Sadiki and Bouandel (2016), likewise, concluded that Tunisia's transition was the most successful, due to a process of concession and democratic consolidation following two elections in 2011 and 2014. Meanwhile, Lebanon has emerged as a unique case study in the Arab Spring, as the confessional power-sharing system became increasingly dysfunctional and fell into several protracted political deadlocks. While there is debate as to whether Lebanon is a frontline Arab Spring country, nevertheless, the Syrian civil war led to a large Syria refugee population in Lebanon and exacerbated political tensions. Moreover, the withdrawal of Syrian troops from Lebanon in 2005, following the Cedar

Revolution, or Spring Revolution, was a precursor to the Arab Spring, and included a significant involvement by women (Stephan 2017, 2018). Indeed, many scholars have noted that gender equality has emerged as an unfinished social revolution, which necessarily follows on from the political revolutions of the Arab Spring (Eltahawy 2015; Khamis and Mili 2017; Stephan 2017, 2018).

SOCIAL MOVEMENT THEORY

This book takes a social movement theory (SMT) perspective to examine the role of women's movements, within the Arab Spring, and the intersectional nature of women's rights and civil rights campaigns in processes of social change. Let us review some key aspects of SMT. Three aspects have been noted regarding the Arab Spring uprisings: they consisted largely of youth, there was significant participation by women, and new media strategies were utilized as modes of communication and mobilization. Yet were these social movements significantly different to those, which have arisen in Western contexts? Social movements first arose in Europe and North America in the late eighteenth century and, at the time, were a new political creation (Tilley and Wood 2009, 3). SMT holds that they include collective claim making that contrasts with someone else's self-interest and engage governments as objects or claimants to achieve those ends. Social movements are conceptualized as a vehicle by which ordinary people participate in public policy and the democratic process, or not. Three elements have been identified in the literature on social movements: first, they are a sustained public effort at collective claims targeting authorities, through the vehicle of a campaign, second, they deploy a combination of political action, such as associations, coalitions, public meetings, rallies, demonstrations, media, and pamphlets as their social movement repertoire, and, finally, they display what are referred to as WUNC: worthiness, unity in numbers, and commitment (Tilley and Wood 2009, 4). Furthermore, Porta and Diani (2006) theorize that social movements are a form of collective action that are conflictual, have clearly identified opponents, are linked by informal networks, and share a distinct collective identity. From these definitions, the Arab Spring uprisings certainly share many features with Western social movements, but a distinctive, unified collective identity is probably the weakest link. Rather, a social movement, which has a diverse informal network, is a more suited conceptual frame.

Moreover, Beinin and Vairel (2013, 1–2) argue that social movements in the Middle East and North Africa (MENA) do not resemble the paradigmatic movements, which formed the basis of SMT, such as the civil rights movement in the American South, the international feminist upsurge of the 1960s and 1970s, or the mobilization of gay and lesbian rights, due to the absence of civil society and democratization in some countries in the region. Nevertheless, they should still be understood as social movements, because:

> The Middle East and North Africa can be understood using the tools that social science has developed for the rest of the world. . . . We argue [it] provides a complex and fascinating laboratory, not only to confirm the applicability of SMT, but also to enrich our theoretical knowledge of social movements and other forms of political contestation.

Consequently, Beinin and Veirel (2013, 3) argue that SMT has neglected the MENA region, or been confined to the analysis of Islamist movements, while secular approaches have been less common in the literature, except for the case of the Israel/Palestine conflict. However, the Arab Spring provides an opportunity to broaden the scope of analysis of SMT to understand the complex nature of the Arab Spring social movements. While they lacked the high degree of cohesion and institutionalization of classical SMT, some Arab Spring countries experienced nonviolent uprisings, such as Tunisia, Egypt, and Lebanon, and others descended into violent conflict, such as Syria, Libya, and Yemen (Beinin and Veirel 2013, 5). Thus, McAdam, Tarrow, and Tilley's *Dynamics of Contention* offers a revised conceptual model, which can be best applied to the MENA context, in which social movements operate against authoritarianisms and are subject to varying degrees of coercion, or even the absence of a state, as is often the case in Lebanon. Hence, social movements in MENA are characterized by weak formal organizations and informal networks, in which process, dynamics and historicized approaches are best suited to understand them (Cited in Beinin and Veirel 2013, 8).

Likewise, the women's movement has long been analyzed by classical SMT, as noted earlier, yet SMT has focused largely on women's rights movements in Western countries, starting in the 1960s and 1970s, while women's movements which emerged in Middle Eastern contexts have been largely neglected, as the next section will show. In fact, women's rights movements in the Middle East share many features with other social movements and are not new to the region, dating back more than a century, to the first wave of feminism in the late nineteenth and early twentieth centuries, a topic this book returns to in chapter 4. Rather, the women's movement is indigenous to the region and addresses local problems and issues that women themselves identify as being important. Stephan (2017, 75) argues that early women's rights advocates in Lebanon, for example, were influenced by the emancipation of Turkish women by Ataturk, before French women even had the right to vote but also by Huda Shaarawi of Egypt, who led the women's movement in Egypt in 1923. I will argue in this book that the fourth wave of the Lebanese women's movement is an extension of previous waves of activism in the MENA region. While not directly causal, the Arab Spring set the context for a period of heightened social movement activism in Lebanon, which has been intersectional in character, combining campaigns for both women's rights and civil rights, leading to political, social, and legal transformation.

Having reviewed SMT literature, it can be argued that the women's movement campaigns, analyzed in this book, demonstrate all three elements of Tilley and Wood's (2009) SMT framework: they are conflictual, linked by informal networks, and probably weakest on the third element, a "collective identity." This is a point that activists themselves identify, due to the structure of sectarian pluralism in Lebanon, and due to the diverse sources of funding for nongovernmental organizations (NGOs), which form the architecture for social movements in Lebanon. In addition to the standard social movement tools, they have adopted online modes of communication and activism, as chapter 5 examines, deploying an iterative movement between online and offline campaign modes to bring about social change. Thus, a key element this book examines is how the fourth wave of the women's movement in Lebanon has extended their campaigns into the online sphere and achieved some degree of success in bringing about legislative change. The period from 2011 to 2019 has seen four key intersectional campaigns that this book will examine to improve women's rights and civil rights, even when the government has been largely absent. Yet the problems and issues, which women's rights campaigners have addressed in Lebanon, are not new but rather represent an enduring puzzle that scholarship on women's rights in the Middle East has returned to time and again.

WOMEN'S RIGHTS SCHOLARSHIP ON THE MIDDLE EAST

Scholars have questioned the status of women in post-Arab Spring societies, from North Africa to Syria, and some have observed that the status of women deteriorated in the aftermath of the Arab Spring revolutions and counterrevolutions (Al-Ali 2012), as controlling women emerged as a key strategy to control communities in times of change. Furthermore, feminist debates over the relationship between citizen's rights and women's rights were revived (Cooke 1994–1995; Cleaver and Wallace 1990). While Mohanty (2011) called for further research into the role of women in the Arab Spring, Wolf (2011) argued that, throughout history, periods of uprising and campaigns for civil rights were followed by campaigns for women's rights, such as the abolitionist and suffragist movements in the United States during the nineteenth century.

Khamis and Mili (2017, 2) write of the Arab Spring revolution/s, or uprisings, as being unfinished and ongoing. Moreover, they argue that gender
issues became prominent early on in the wave of sociopolitical change,
because, first, women were active in the course of the revolutions, as was the
case in Egypt and Tunisia and Lebanon and elsewhere, and second, their participation redefined gendered spaces and confirmed women's agency, while
not confining them to traditional gender roles supporting men. Consequently,
women merged the "struggle for equal citizenship and full participation in
the political sphere with that of greater gender equality in the social arena"
(Khamis and Mili 2017, 3). Thus, while men fought one political struggle,
women fought two parallel struggles: one to end political injustice and the
other to end social injustice, according to Khamis and Mili (2017, 3). For
example, in the course of constitutional reform, in the aftermath of the Arab
Spring, the role of women in private and public space became central to the
political debate between liberal and Islamist constitutional traditions, as was
the case in Tunisia (Khamis and Mili 2017, 3). Throughout the region, Khamis and Mili (2017) argue, there is a need to tackle the underlying structures
of injustice, which negatively impact Arab women, politically, socially, and
legally. Consequently, they revisit intersectionality in feminist theory, within
an Arab context. Rather than women being situated at the intersection of
multiple sources of oppression, as such, Khamis and Mili (2017, 6) argue we
need to consider how Arab women oscillate between binary opposites, such
as tradition and modernity, private and public, the religious and secular. Thus,
Arab women are caught at the crossroads between political, social, and legal
struggles, a point of view this book shares.

Similarly, Eltahawy (2015, 5) argues that the Middle East needs a sexual
revolution to follow the political revolution initiated by the Arab Spring. She
finds that the political struggle has led to an unfinished gender struggle. While
opponents may contend that basic political rights should be achieved before
women's rights, she does not agree. Rather, she proposes that gender equality should be an integral part of the Arab Spring transformation. She points
to the high level of street harassment in many countries, as a case in point,
the low level of female representation in government, low female labor force
participation across the region, and restrictive mobility laws, as indicators of
women's untapped potential across the region. Like Khamis and Mili (2017),
she maintains that a second sexual revolution must follow the political revolution inspired by the Arab Spring, in order to free "half the population" from
their status as dependents: "it is our chance to dismantle the entire political
and economic system, if not now then when?"

However, Cooke (2016) warns that Arab feminists must heed the "Algerian lesson," whereby women were included in the struggle for the Algerian
revolution, when they were "needed" but excluded when it was "all over" and

sent back to the domestic sphere. Today, she argues, activists have moved from euphoria, to backlash and persistence in the aftermath of the Arab Spring. While the tensions between women's rights and civil rights have long been the subject of feminist scholarship globally (Lyons 2004; Peteet and American Council of Learned Societies. 1991; O'Gorman 2011; Cleaver and Wallace 1990b; Chung and Kaarsholm 2006; Badran and Cooke 1990; Cooke 1988; 1994–1995; Al-Ali 2000), the social movements of the Arab Spring have revived the debate.

The field of Middle East women's studies predates the so-called Arab Spring (Joseph 1996a; Charrad 2001; Al-Rasheed 2013; Coleman 2013; Ahmed 1992; Arenfeldt and Al-Hassan Golley 2012; Al-Ali 2000; Abu-Lughod 2013). Scholars have examined women's rights movements dating back to the early twentieth century, prior to independence, throughout the region (Badran and Cooke 1990), as noted earlier. Overall, Charrad (2011a, 418) has identified four key themes, within the field of gender in the Middle East. First, the critique of Orientalism, following Said (1978), whereby the Middle East is represented as exotic, bound by tradition and inferior to the West. Rather, Middle East women scholars focus on the crisis of Western representation and the importance of Arab women putting their viewpoints and arguments forward, in their own terms. Second, scholars paint a more complex picture, which recognizes the diversity of interpretations within the Islamic tradition, which is not monolithic, noting the four main schools of Islamic law, which chapter 3 examines. Third, a recognition of the role of kinship in states, as well as the extended family and patriarchy, in defining gender ideologies. Fourth, studies which recognize the agency of Arab women in social life and organizations, rather than representing Arab women as victims, and finally, the role of Islamic feminism and the meaning of veiling.

From this overview of the field, this study draws on three intertwined strands of scholarship. First, historical studies focused on the antecedents of women's status in the region and the evolution of patriarchy and family law (Ahmed 1992; Charrad 2001; Joseph 1996; Thompson 2000). Second, studies with a secular approach to the studies of women's rights movements (Al-Ali 2000), and finally, studies which examine the potential of Islamic feminism to bring about social change (Mahmood 2005; Mernissi 1987; Abu-Lughod 2013). Moreover, Keddie (2006) identifies a contradiction within Middle East women's studies between universalists and relativists, derived from their approach to the question of Middle East women's rights. The former emphasize women's studies in all disciplines and take a universalist approach to women's equality, irrespective of the context, drawing on international instruments and human rights charters. The relativists, or Third World feminists, by contrast, emphasize Islamic specificity and difference. A *rapprochement*, she argues, is for studies to recognize their historical context and to take a dialectical approach, rather than a dichotomous approach. A more nuanced perspective would situate practices, in their specific past or present context, and emphasize women's agency, as well as structure and representation.

Following the relativist approach, a central theme of scholarship on women's rights in the Middle East is the relationship between citizenship rights, personal status law, patriarchy, and the role of women's movements in processes of reform. Joseph (1996b) notes that, throughout the Middle East, women are depicted as icons for nations but are subject to patriarchal structures and ideologies, which privilege males and elders through kinship. Moreover, she argues, that personal status laws, which regulate marriage, divorce, inheritance, and child custody, are the key mode by which Middle Eastern states incorporate subnational communities and religious sects into "juridical communities" and regulate women's sexuality to reproduce both sect and nation (Joseph 1996, 7). All Middle Eastern countries, except for Turkey and Tunisia, she notes, defer personal status issues to legally recognized religious authorities.

Following the universalist approach to women's rights, the dual positioning of women's rights movements in non-Western societies is evident. Al-Ali's (2000, 22–27) pioneering study on secularism and the Egyptian women's movement noted the dual positioning of women's rights movements in postcolonial societies between Orientalism and Occidentalism and the struggle of women's rights activists for authenticity in the face of criticism from both conservative Islamist and left-wing nationalists forces (Al-Ali 2000, 32–32). Indeed, Al-Ali (2000, 4) explains that secular women's rights activists do not endorse *Shari'a* (Islamic law) as the main source of legislation but refer to civil law and human rights conventions, as stipulated by the United Nations, as frameworks for their struggles (Al-Ali 2000, 33). For Al-Ali, secularism is "an acceptance of a separation between religion and politics." Associated with the rise of the modern state, secularism achieves a transcendent mediation by overcoming the "particular and differentiating practices of the self that are articulated through class, gender and religion through the medium of citizenship," based upon an individual conception of the human citizen/subject, a civil legal code, and a secular state (Al-Ali 2000, 13). Citizenship is the sum total of legal obligations and entitlements individuals possess by virtue of membership to a nation state and the practices through which individuals and groups obtain and expand their rights (Al-Ali 2000).

By contrast, following the relativist or Third World approach, Abu-Lughod (2013) argues that Muslim women do not need saving. Rather, international organizations and transnational women's movements have unduly focused on the victim status of Middle Eastern women, to the detriment of recognizing their agency and the political and economic nature of their struggles. Indeed, for relativist authors, Western feminism has taken an imperialist turn in the post-9/11 era and imposed a Western representation of Middle Eastern women's second-class position, by focusing unduly on Islamic law, as the primary source of women's inequality, reproducing an "orientalist trope" and missing the role of patriarchy in other religious traditions in the Middle East. Rather, Abu-Lughod cautions against accounts, which overlook complexities and differences, in analyses of women's rights but also create a binary between universalist rights, on the one hand, and culture/religion, on the other (Abu-Lughod 2013, 219–226). Rather, Abu-Lughod (2013) paints a more nuanced and complex picture of the relationship between women's rights, law, and states, in times of change in the Middle East but also the representation of these processes to Western audiences.

Islamic feminism can be defined as "a feminist discourse and practice articulated within an Islamic paradigm," according to Badran (2009, 242). It offers feminist interpretations of key religious texts and the possibility of an indigenous Middle Eastern feminism (Badran 2005; Mernissi 1987). Another theorist, Hussein (2016), focuses on the intersection between the West and East and between Muslim majority and minority societies. She writes of the struggles facing Muslim women living in the West after 9/11 (Hussein 2016), highlighting the white supremacist context, whereby sexism and racism are intertwined and Muslim women's "cultural practices" are pathologized. The "veil" has become a visual representation of Islam in societies consumed by Islamophobia. Right-wing movements in Western countries consistently pathologize Islam as an inherently "backward" religion, because women do not have rights. In counterpoint, Islamic feminist activists argue that women have rights in Islam, in relation to divorce and property for instance; the problem is in the implementation. Moreover, the problem is cultural, not religious, because patriarchy is pervasive, a point this book returns to in chapter 3 in the discussion of personal status law in Lebanon.

In any case, universalist approaches need to take into consideration the context in which women rights activists are struggling, as it frames the nature of the struggle and the order of priorities. For instance, has the society in question institutionalized religious difference within a system of legal pluralism, such as Lebanon, secularized the national laws by separating religion and politics, such as Australia, or adopted an overarching religion of state, such as Saudi Arabia? Following, Keddie's (2006) proposal, this study takes a dialectical approach, which bridges the binary between the universalists and relativists in Middle East women's studies, by examining the historical context, the complexity in family law traditions, and the importance of analyzing kinship, sect, and the state, in the case of Lebanon.

ANTHROPOLOGY, LEGAL PLURALISM,
AND SECULARISM

The tensions between plural and national approaches to law are a question that legal anthropology has long examined (Nader 2002, 271), with the key message being that "Western jurisprudential ideas will not do as categories for use in comparing 'non-Western' cultures." Rather, how are disputes negotiated in systems with multiple systems of jurisprudence? The intersection between legal systems has also been examined, as well as how dispute resolution systems intersect (Humphrey 1989), and which models can best represent plural societies in multicultural contexts (Nichols 2012a). Other scholars have examined the anthropology of secularism (Asad 2003), and asked whether secularism is inherently a Western concept, which cannot be easily mapped onto non-Western contexts. Saba Mahmood (2016) has argued, for instance, in the case of the Coptic Orthodox Christians, a minority in Egypt, that the persistence of religious-based family laws in the Middle East is a result of a partial secularization process, which privatized religious power within the family, while other aspects of life came to be governed by civil law. However, in so doing, the family became the locus of control (Mahmood 2016, 114).

In many postcolonial states, the major religions coexist and customary laws and civil laws have both been adopted, as parallel systems, or national systems of family law have developed, while the personal status laws of minority religions have been retained, such as the case of India. Integrating both religious and civil law systems is always challenging and an enduring puzzle, which has two aspects: first, how can the state institutionalize religious difference in a plural society and, second, how can the state in plural societies maintain a national system of law, which provides equal rights to all citizens? One solution is to institutionalize secular, national laws, which institutionalize the separation of religion and politics, as is common in liberal democracies in Western countries, as noted earlier, resulting in minority religions, which are not recognized. The other is to institutionalize religious difference, within a plural legal and political system, as is the case in Lebanon's consociational system of government and law but at the expense of equal citizenship rights for men or women, the dynamics of which this book explores.

Moreover, the process on secularization and modernization has not followed a linear process in the Middle East. Charrad's (2011b, 50) work has shown that kinship has formed an important part of the formation of states in the Middle East and influenced the institutionalization of religious family law, as chapter 3 examines. Moreover, in state-building processes a complex relationship emerges between states and local communities to exert control over territory, which she refers to as patrimonialism. Consequently, state-building processes have not exhibited a linear trajectory toward secularization and centralization in many Middle Eastern states but rather an interplay between patrimonialism, based on personal ties, and central state authority.

Associated with the rise of the modern state, secularism, according to Asad (2003), overcomes the "particular and differentiating practices of the self that are articulated through class, gender and religion" through the medium of citizenship (Asad 2003, 5). Yet the link between secularization, citizenship, and democratization is not clear in the Middle East, according to Sadiki (2004, 165), who posits that it has become an Orientalist trope, which does not account for "cross-national or cultural differences." Moreover, he cautions, state-led secularism is not achievable when Islamic particularism permeates everyday life. The secularization thesis (Dobbelaere 1999) hypothesizes a link between modernization, political rationalization, and the decline of religion in public life, but according to Sadiki it is an exception in the Middle East, as is French-style political secularism, *laïcité*.[1] Rather, Sadiki (2004, 165) observes a process of secularization and sacralization occurring concurrently, alongside democratic transition, with a blurring of the boundaries between the two processes. Lebanon provides such a case study: with a hybrid legal and political system it combines civil and religious laws, while recognizing the personal status law of eighteen recognized religious communities; however, women's rights remain relational and contingent.

THE WOMEN'S RIGHTS PUZZLE IN LEBANON

This study examines the implications of Lebanon's consociational system of political and legal pluralism for women's rights and asks, *is secular citizenship the key to solving the women's rights puzzle in Lebanon?* In this book, I am interested in how women's rights activists, who reside in Lebanon, frame their campaigns for social change and gender justice and the issues they identify as being important sites of struggle, in particular the system of plural religious family law, which is unique within the Middle Eastern context, as it mediates citizenship status. I apply a dialectical approach, which combines all three approaches identified in the literature on Middle Eastern women's rights scholarship, to understand the nature of the women's rights puzzle in Lebanon and I apply SMT to examine four contemporary women's rights campaigns in Lebanon. While the majority of Middle Eastern states are Muslim majority societies, Lebanon is unusual in the region, in that the system of legal pluralism recognizes eighteen religious sects, including Muslims, Christians, and Jews, which are governed by fifteen personal status courts (Mikdashi 2014). Furthermore, citizenship laws in Lebanon deny women nationality rights, as nationality rights are passed to children through patrilineal descent from one's father, or husband. In the Lebanese case, therefore, women experience discrimination under both religious and civil law, because they have what Joseph (1996b, 9) terms relational rights, which are mediated through their significant relationships with others, in particular their husband and father. Furthermore, Mikdashi (2014, 281), proposes that both gender and sect need to be considered in relation to personal status, civil, criminal, and procedural laws in Lebanon, as sources of women's differential status.

While the Lebanese model of confessional democracy is based on a consociational division of power between Catholics, Orthodox Christians, Sunnis, Shi'ites, and Druze, as noted earlier, it institutionalizes religious difference in both private relationships and politics. I argue that the system of legal dualism is the source of the women's rights deficit in Lebanon, because women are caught between their religious affiliation and their citizenship status. Why? First, women do not have full nationality rights, but rather, they have relational citizenship rights, thus they are unable to pass their nationality onto their children if they are not married to a Lebanese husband. Second, there is no unified civil status code for matters of personal status, rather sectarian affiliation, determines women's differential access to marriage, divorce, maintenance, inheritance, and child custody rights. Thus, a dual legal system separates religious law from civil law and locates family law within religious law and all matters of personal status are governed by the religious court of the respective confession, with limited oversight (Human Rights Watch 2015). Lastly, the confessional system is reproduced through the institution of marriage, whereby sectarian affiliation is privileged over the development of a unified national identity, through the logic of patrilineal descent, leaving women's citizenship status as contingent and ambiguous.

METHODOLOGY

This book presents the findings of phase one, two, and three of the research project "Beyond Sect: The Lebanese Women's Movement and the Search for Secular Citizenship in the Arab Spring." The first stage of the mixed methods research design (Bryman and Bell 2011, 627) in 2012 drew on a qualitative research strategy. Through purposeful sampling (Berg 2009, 50), thirty interviewees were recruited from across the spectrum of Lebanese women's organizations to participate in semi-structured, in-depth interviews. The interview guide explored key issues relating to digital media technologies, including use patterns, consumption, and digital divide issues, as well as the application of digital media technology for women's activism. The interviews were digitally recorded and transcribed, de-identified, coded, and analyzed thematically (Bryman and Bell 2011, 586) using the computer-assisted software package

NVivo. The second quantitative stage of the research design in 2013 distributed an online survey, through the email and Facebook networks of the Lebanese women's movement in order to collect generalizable data on social media use and to rank-order the most pressing women's rights issues in Lebanon and 110 completed surveys were returned. Phase three of the research design examined the civil marriage debate in Lebanon and undertook twenty face-to-face interviews with civil marriage couples and activists and circulated an online civil marriage attitudes survey through email networks and Facebook; the survey was also advertised on the webpage of the Institute for Women's Studies at the Lebanese American University (now Arab Institute for Women AiW) and 160 surveys were completed. The data from all three phases of the research design were triangulated to validate the research findings presented in this book.

CHAPTER OUTLINE

This book has two parts. The first part of the book, *Formations*, examines political and legal origins and foundations of the Lebanese consociational system in chapters 1 and 2. The second part of the book, *Activism*, in chapters 4–7, examines the rise of the Lebanese women's movement and a new wave of activism, which accelerated after 2011.

Part I: Formations

Chapter 2 examines the antecedents of the formation of Lebanon's system of consociational power sharing, referred to as a confessional democracy, which divides political power between eighteen recognized religious sects. The chapter starts with a discussion of the location of Lebanon as an historic refuge for heterodox religious minorities (Salibi 1988), due to its mountainous terrain, unique climate, and location at the crossroads between the East and West. The chapter then discusses the emergence of the *Mutasarrifate*, or a semiautonomous region, within the Ottoman Empire and the impact of the decline of Ottoman power during the arrival of European powers in the region and formation of the French Mandate, which saw a shift toward institutionalizing religious difference, formalized in the National Pact of 1943, at the time of Lebanon's independence. While Christians received a higher proportion of seats than Muslims in parliament, at the time of independence from the French, the ratio was later revised to parity, in the aftermath of the Lebanese Civil War of 1975–1990. The machinations of the power-sharing system and the relative balance between the sects have been at the core of struggles in Lebanon since the French Mandate. While Traboulsi (2012, vii) theorizes that two distinctive features have had a significant impact on the formation of modern Lebanon, first, a sizeable Christian population, and second, a long exposure to the West. The former, he argues, led to the insti-tutionalization of religious sects, or sectarianism, and the latter to Lebanon's economic liberalization and a problematic relationship between Lebanon and the Middle Eastern region. However, I argue that a third key element should be considered, the implications of Lebanon's confessional power-sharing system for gender relations, and vice versa, and the important role regulating women's sexuality, through the institution of marriage, plays in the reproduction of sect and nation, as evidenced by women's relational citizenship rights and the loca-tion of family law within religious law, respectively. Looking across Lebanese history, a continuity can be seen between the dynamics of difference, on the one hand, and struggle for state formation and a national identity, on the other.

Chapter 3 examines Lebanon's complex system of legal pluralism and the evolution of the division between civil and religious law, dating back to the French Mandate. While the Ottomans developed the *millet* system, whereby non-Muslim religious subjects were governed in accordance with their faith, this mode of governing religious difference was codified into fifteen sepa-rate personal status codes for eighteen recognized religious confessions in Lebanon during the French Mandate. This chapter examines how the personal status codes were developed and the system of family law, which operates in Lebanon today. The chapter starts by discussing the anthropology of marriage systems and the trend toward the democratization of personal relationships and marriage. The chapter then examines the differences between the Chris-tian and Muslim personal status codes and the differential access to marriage, divorce, and child custody rights for women across all personal status codes.

Part II: Activism

Chapter 4 examines the upsurge in women's rights campaigns in Lebanon, the start of the Arab Spring in 2011, and the role of women among the new social movements. While the critical role of new media technologies in facili-tating new social movements has been widely debated, fewer studies have collected empirical data on online campaigns in the Arab uprisings or asked activists themselves their views on the efficacy of online versus offline modes of social mobilization. This chapter contributes to the conversation by com-paring online and offline women's rights activism in Lebanon, and examining movements that employ both modes of social mobilization. It asks, has new media technology enabled the Lebanese women's movement to enter a new and more radical phase in its development? Through analyzing the online/offline activism to introduce a law that criminalizes domestic violence in April 2014, my findings suggest that no one mode of activism was superior over the other. Rather, I propose that the iterative dynamism between the two modes of activism has led to significant reforms.

Chapter 5 discusses the intersection between women's rights campaigns in Lebanon and broader social and political movements that have emerged in the last five years. The campaigns overlap and address a broad array of social and political grievances that Lebanese have experienced with the state, or its absence. From women's nationality rights, to electoral reform and the #YouStink garbage campaigns, at the height of Lebanon's garbage crisis in 2015, the campaigns show the intersection between the women's rights deficit and the deadlock in Lebanon's political system. The chapter examines the links between these seemingly disparate campaigns and the extended political deadlock in Lebanon's government, which focus on bringing political reforms, improve women's representation, address gender-based violence, the problem of sectarianism, and ecological crises arising from the protracted political deadlock.

Chapter 6 considers the movement for civil marriage reform, as part of the Lebanese women's movement's campaign for comprehensive personal status law reform and the adoption of a unified civil status code. While chapter 5 considers the intersection between the Lebanese women's movement and civil society campaigns for political reform of the voting system, nationality rights, women's electoral representation, and public administration, chapter 6 considers perhaps the most contentious issue facing women's rights in Lebanon, the reform of the plural system of personal status law, as embodied in the civil marriage debate in Lebanon. The debate raises important questions regarding women's location between sect and nation in Lebanon, due to the absence of a civil marriage law and differential personal status codes, as outlined in chapter 3, for all matters relating to marriage, divorce, maintenance, inheritance, and child custody. The recognition of Lebanon's first civil marriage contracted in 2013 reignited the national debate, as a new generation of activists sought the recognition of civil marriage before the courts. This chapter starts by defining civil marriage in the Lebanese context; it then examines the argument for civil marriage, examines the argument against the recognition of civil marriage, and then analyzes the motivations of three case study civil marriage couples to understand their reasons for seeking a civil marriage. The chapter concludes with a consideration of the implications of the civil marriage debate for the women's rights puzzle in Lebanon.

Chapter 7 returns to the book's thesis: women are caught between sect and nation in Lebanon, because of Lebanon's plural legal system, which restricts women's nationality rights and defers women to their religious confession for all matters of personal status. Women are caught between their religious affiliation and their citizenship status, which renders some of them stateless and restricts others' rights in marriage and divorce. Thus, to improve women's rights, the book concludes that the marriage contract needs to be rewritten to provide an optional civil code. Moreover, the consociational system restricts women's nationality rights, as well as marriage and divorce rights, for the primacy of sect, as a mode of social reproduction, identification, and political representation.

CONCLUSION

This introduction situated this study within the literature on new social movements in the Arab Spring, Middle East women's studies, and legal anthropology. The chapter examined significant debates in Middle East women's studies, noting the differences between the universalists and relativists and the importance of a dialectical approach. The chapter asked whether secularism is a Western concept and noted that state formation, secularism, and modernity follow a nonlinear trajectory in the Middle East. The chapter then examined the women's rights puzzle in Lebanon, whereby women are caught between sect and nation, due to the consociational power-sharing system between eighteen recognized religious confessions. The chapter then outlined the methodology applied in this study to answer the research questions and the structure of the book, as well as the key women's rights campaigns it will examine. Let us now turn to the origins of Lebanon's system of confessional democracy.

NOTES

1. Apart from the Middle Eastern region, the United States is the other notable exception to the secularization thesis, because the U.S. Constitution enshrines religious freedom and the practice of religious affiliation has been rising, not declining.

Chapter 2

The Formation of Lebanon as a Confessional Democracy

An Accommodation of Difference?

INTRODUCTION

This chapter examines the antecedents of the formation of Lebanon's system of consociational power sharing, referred to as a confessional democracy, which divides political power between eighteen recognized religious sects. The chapter starts with a discussion of the location of Lebanon as a historic refuge for heterodox religious minorities (Salibi 1988), due to its mountainous terrain, unique climate, and location at the crossroads between East and West. The chapter then discusses the emergence of the *Mutasarrifate*, a semiautonomous region within the Ottoman Empire, and the arrival of European powers in the region. The formation of the French Mandate, following the collapse of the Ottoman Empire, at the end of World War I, saw a new order emerge in the institutionalization of religious difference, formalized in the National Pact of 1943, at the time of Lebanon's independence. While Christians received a higher proportion of seats in parliament than Muslims did, the ratio was later revised to parity after the Lebanese Civil War of 1975–1990. The machinations of the power-sharing system and the relative balance between the sects have been at the core of political struggles in Lebanon since the French Mandate. Moreover, Traboulsi (2012, vii) theorizes that two distinctive features influenced the formation of modern Lebanon, first, a sizeable Christian population, and second, a long exposure to the West. The former, he argues, led to the institutionalization of religious sects, and the latter led to Lebanon's economic liberalization, as well as a problematic relationship between Lebanon and the Middle Eastern region. However, I argue a third key element should be considered, the impact of Lebanon's confessional power-sharing system on gender relations and, conversely, the role of the institution of marriage in the reproduction of sect and nation. Looking across Lebanese history, a continuous interplay can be traced between the dynamics of religious difference, on the one hand, and the struggle for state formation and a unified national identity, on the other. Women's rights are caught between the two imperatives.

A HISTORIC REFUGE

Lebanon is located in the Eastern Mediterranean (see map 1) and borders Syria and Israel. There are three main geographical regions: the coastal plain, the Lebanon Range, and the Anti-Lebanon Range, with the Beqaa valley in between. The highest mountain, Jabal Lubnan (Mont Liban), at 3,500 meters, is part of the Lebanon Ranges and generates significant rainfall, approximately 82.5 centimeters annually, providing a fertile agricultural climate in a region dominated by desert (Hitti 1965, 11–12). The Lebanese mountains historically provided refuge for Lebanon's diverse religious groupings, a historical feature of mountainous regions in precapitalist societies, according to Hage (1989, 129). Moreover, Lebanon has eighteen recognized religious sects and minorities, which comprise, but are not limited to, Sunni and Shi'ite Muslims, Alawites, Ismaili's, and Druze[1] and Eastern rite Christians including Maronite, Greek, Armenian and Syrian Catholics (Melkites), Syrian Jocobites, Greek Orthodox, Coptics, Nestorians, and Jews (Cobban 1985, 15). Lebanon's proximity to the Fertile Crescent and its central location in the Eastern Mediterranean has placed it at the crossroads of a series of empires throughout history including the Canaanite/Phoenician, Mesopotamian, Persian, Hellenistic, Roman, Christian Byzantine, Islamic, Crusader, Mamluk, Ottoman, and finally, the colonial French (Cobban 1985, 70).

THE OTTOMAN EMPIRE

The Ottoman Empire had a long-term and significant presence in Lebanon from 1521 to 1918, which then was part of the province of Syria, until the empire collapsed at the end of World War I (Batrouney 1985, 12). The Ottoman Empire encapsulated all of the Arabic-speaking people of the Middle East and extended into the Balkans in Eastern Europe, North Africa, and to the Arabian Gulf, including the holy cities of Islam in the *Hijaz* (Lewis 1997). The Ottoman Empire was a multiethnic and multireligious empire, which left a legacy on the formation of Lebanon's political and family law system. Due to Sunni Islam being the religion of state, "religions of the book" were recognized as minority religions through the administration of the *millet* system, which institutionalized parallel personal status codes for minorities, including Christians and Jews (and Hindus under Islamic empires further to the East). Non-Muslims were recognized as *dhimmis*; under Islamic law, while they could practice their religion, they paid a poll tax (the *jizya*) in exchange for protection. Other restrictions applied to dress and the building of places of worship. According to Hourani (1991), the Islamic laws of marriage and inheritance were strictly observed throughout the Islamic empires of the Middle East, including in the Ottoman Empire. As such:

> A non-Muslim could not inherit from a Muslim; a non-Muslim man could not marry a Muslim woman, but a Muslim man could marry a Jewish or Christian women. Conversion of Muslims to other religions was strictly forbidden. (Hourani 1991, 117)

Separate personal status codes, thus, applied to non-Muslims across the Ottoman Empire. In the later decades of the Ottoman Empire, *millet* also applied to Muslims communities.[2] The legacy of the *millet* system laid the basis for the development of modern Lebanon's dual legal system, due to the presence of a significant Christian population; however, parallel personal status codes also applied to Muslim confessions, a topic examined further in the next chapter.

If isolation and an austere way of life were historical features of the Maronites of Mount Lebanon, as a Christian minority in an Islamic region, their fortunes changed with the arrival of French imperialism in the region in the nineteenth century. At the time, Mount Lebanon fell under the jurisdiction of the *Pasha* (governor) of Saida (Sidon). Below the *Pasha* was the *Emir* of the mountain, from the *Shihab* dynasty, who collected taxes on behalf of the Ottomans. The most notable *Shihab* Emir was Bashir II (1788–1840) who consolidated control over the mountain (Salibi 1971, 77). Below the *Emir* were the Druze lords, referred to as *Muqata'jis*, who were large landowners in the system of feudal property relations referred to as *Iqta*. The peasantry was divided between *Mutayers*, landless serfs, who worked the land of the *Muqata'jis* and what Salibi terms the "free peasantry," who owned small plots and paid tribute, many of whom were Maronites (Salibi 1971; Hage 1989, 136–137).

The power relations between Muslims and Christians began to change in the late 1800s with the arrival of the European powers, which competed for the domination of trade in the region throughout the nineteenth century, with the main rivals being the British and the French. Part of their strategy was to make alliances with local sectarian groupings and to become their "protectors." The British were allied with the Druze, the Russians with the Orthodox Christians, and the French with the Maronites (Russell 1985, 17). Hage

(1989, 213) links the Maronite ascendancy to their alliance with the French and their subsequent domination of the silk trade, through the development of a Maronite bourgeoisie class. This led to four key historical features of Maronite self-identification: their intrinsic difference from their surroundings, their superiority over the "Muslim other," fear, and the need for protection. He links these key features of the Maronite identity to what he terms the "fetishism of identity." The Maronites perceived their sectarian identity, as Christians, to be the source of their "superiority" and difference from the Muslim other. Maronite difference also developed into a form of colonial whiteness, a self-perception of being white like the French (Hage 2004, 188). For the French, their alliance with the Maronites was a means to achieve their colonial designs in the Middle East. A power struggle developed between the Druze, whose power derived from their position as *Muqata'jis* in the *Iqta* system of feudalism, and the Maronites, due to their alliance with the French. Hage (1989, 203) argues this led to the subsequent exclusion of the Druze from the silk industry. This culminated in the civil war of 1860, in which a Maronite peasant revolt was suppressed by the Druze lords and thousands of Christians were slaughtered and their silk crops destroyed (Batrouney 1985, 4).

Consequently, the Ottoman rulers, under pressure from the European powers to protect the "Christians," were forced to administer Mount Lebanon as a semiautonomous region, referred to as the *Mutasarrifate*, or provincial governorship, after 1861 (Salibi 1971, 78). The chief administrator was to be a *Mutasarrif*, or governor, and was to be a non-Lebanese Ottoman subject of Catholic background. A local administrative council was to advise him and its membership was to be fixed with four Maronite members, three Druze, two Greek Orthodox, and one each from the Greek Catholic, Sunni, and Shi'ite communities. This was the early model for the modern confessional state in Lebanon (Cobban 1985, 51). While the *Mutasarrifate* comprised a Christian majority at the time, many of whom saw it as a Maronite homeland and a prototype for future state of their own (Salibi 1971, 78–79), that is not how it worked out.

THE FRENCH MANDATE

Following the collapse of the Ottoman Empire after World War I, the French received a mandate from the League of Nations over the territory of present-day Lebanon and Syria. A push emerged among Christian nationalists for the formation of a Maronite nation and, according to Hage (1989, 218), "For the Maronite subject, the nation had to be, if not an exclusively Christian nation, at least, a nation for the Christians." This imagined Maronite nation was not supported by all the Maronites, however, in particular the Beiruti/French capitalist class who saw it as too isolationist, as their trading interests and those of the French included both Mount Lebanon and the Muslim interior (Hage 1989, 222). Furthermore, the boundaries of the *Mutasarrifate* were considered unviable for a functioning state because:

> The territorial limits of the *Mutasarrifate* . . . deprived the country of ports for its commerce and suitable land for its agriculture. . . . Lebanon . . . could not develop to its full potential unless its territory was enlarged to include the coastal cities of Tripoli, Beirut, Sidon, and Tyre, along with the *Beqaa* and the plain of *Akkar*, to the north of *Tripoli*. (Salibi 1971, 79)

The borders of the modern state of Lebanon were, thus, changed to include the coastal cities of Tyre, Sidon, Beirut, and Tripoli. In so doing, the demographic balance between Christians and Muslims was altered, from the formula applied in the *Mutasarrifate*, which laid the foundations for the recurrent problems balancing the power-sharing formula with the demographic realities of the polity. However, the problems went further.

The modern state of Lebanon, created during the French Mandate in 1926, was separated from the territory of greater Syria. Moreover, the French Mandate saw the establishment of a new constitutional order, which reversed the order of confessional power that prevailed under the Ottomans, when:

> privilege extended down from those who received the most benefits, state official themselves, to Muslim elites in major cities, to potential (male) recruits for military and civil service, and lastly, to non-Muslims, women, workers and peasants. (Thompson 2000, 76)

Through the development of Western education, led by missionaries, free trade through the Port of Beirut, and "special protection" for Christians, the French Mandate turned the Ottoman order on its head. In the new social hierarchy, which resulted from their "civilizing mission," including education, social and health policies, as well as employment in state jobs, a new tacit pecking order emerged. Christians disproportionately accessed the civil service: "not only for political reasons, but simply because more of them were schooled in French schools, so knew French" (Thompson 2000, 81). Meanwhile, Greek Orthodox and Catholics dominated the banking and commercial sectors. From the beginning, Sunni Muslims protested their relative exclusion from state jobs and economic benefits, while Shi'ites were situated at the bottom of the new tacit order (Thompson 2000, 81). The emerging state, thus, contained the seeds of discontent beneath the surface appearance of a liberal democratic order, because underlying the confessional labels and perceived inequities persisted, such that, according to Salibi, "Greater Lebanon . . . was truly a statue of guilded bronze standing on feet of clay" (Salibi 1988, 66).

INDEPENDENCE

In 1943 Lebanon gained independence from the French and its constitution was formalized under the National Pact of 1943 (Cobban 1985, 70; Humphrey 1998, 65). Lebanon's system of confessional democracy allocates political power on the basis of religious sect, as determined by the population distribution determined in the 1932[3] census (Salibi 1988). Under the division of power determined by the National Pact the president is a Maronite Catholic, the prime minister, a Sunni Muslim, and the speaker of the house, a Shi'ite, while the deputy speaker is a Christian Orthodox. In the original formula, 128 seats in parliament were divided on a 6-to-5 ratio in favor of Christians over Muslims; however, the 1989 Ta'if Accord, which ended the civil war, revised the ratio to parity (Traboulsi 2012, 107). While the Lebanese state divides political power between three major religious sects, Maronite Catholics, Sunni Muslims, and Shi'ite Muslims, Lebanon recognizes a total of eighteen religious sects, as noted above. Yet, the power-sharing arrangement, according to Traboulsi (2012, 110–111), institutionalized the political, economic, and social primacy of the Maronites, as enshrined by their allocation of the presidency, while the Sunni's were allocated the role of prime minister and the Shi'ite's the role of speaker of the house. While, at the time of independence, Christians were estimated to comprise 75 percent of the population (Salibi 1971, 84), as noted in the preface, they are now thought to be 37 percent of the population (Economist 2016), due to a century of emigration, in which Christians outnumbered Muslims. The arrival of two major refugee populations in Lebanon, the Palestinians who were displaced from the formation of Israel in 1948, who now number more than 500,000 people, and more than 1 million Syrian refugees since 2011,[4] has further shifted the demographic balance in favor of Muslims. Furthermore, no national census has been conducted since 1932 to substantiate the change, or to revise the power-sharing formula accordingly (Traboulsi, 2012).

THE CIVIL WAR AND ITS AFTERMATH

Efforts to alter or abolish the confessional system have been at the center of Lebanese politics for decades. Those sects most favored by the National Pact sought to preserve it, while those who saw themselves at a disadvantage sought, either to revise the power allocation by updating key demographic data, or to abolish the National Pact entirely, and this became the basis for the Lebanese Civil War of 1975–1990 (Russell 1985, 17). The spark which started the civil war commenced in April 1975, following a shooting in front of a Greek Orthodox church in East Beirut. However, economic inequality also played a role in the conflict. The laissez-faire Lebanese system had entrenched wealth and political power in the hands of a few elite landowning and merchant families, who were predominantly Christian, referred to as "The Four Percent Class," and they controlled 32 percent of the country's gross domestic product (Russell 1985, 18; Batrouney 1992, 18).

But, the multifaceted conflict centered not only on the distribution of political and economic power, it also went to the heart of the Lebanese identity and the history of the country (Salibi 1988). Did Lebanon have a unique history as a refuge for minorities, based on a Christian specificity and a Phoenician identity, or should Lebanon look to a pan-Arab nationalism for its identity? Referred to as a "war of others," the involvement of external actors and powers in the conflict, such as Palestinians, Syrians, and Americans, as well as the Arab Israeli conflict, all were partly blamed (Fisk 2002). Other analysts, meanwhile, focused on the internal dynamics between nonstate actors, which contributed to the war, including the confessional contradictions of the National Pact (Salibi 1988). Nevertheless, the country divided along two broad fighting coalitions: the Lebanese National Movement (LNM), which comprised predominantly Lebanese Muslim and Palestinian factions, and the Lebanese Forces (LF), which comprised Lebanese Christian factions, including the Phalange. While it is beyond this short history to provide an exhaustive account of the war, the fighting went through three broad phases. The first phase was the outbreak of the war in 1975–1976, when the Syrian army intervened. The second broad phase was from 1977 to 1982, including the rise of Bashir Gemayel to the presidency, his subsequent assassination, and the Israeli invasion and occupation of Beirut, which resulted in the expulsion of the PLO from Lebanon. The last phase of the war was from 1983 to 1990, which concluded with intra-Christian fighting between General Aoun, the then head of the armed forces, and the LF militia (Traboulsi 2012). In total, the fighting continued for fifteen years and resulted in the death of 71,328 people, while 97,184 people were injured. Moreover, the war resulted in three kinds of demographic purges, according to Traboulsi (2012, 244). First, sectarian cleansing, which created religiously homogeneous enclaves, as a result of expulsing Shi'ite Muslims from Christian areas and Christians from the Druze mountain. Altogether 157,000 Muslims and 670,000 Christians were displaced. Second, the expulsion of "foreigners," principally Palestinians, because of the Israeli invasion and the massacres at Sabra-Shatila Palestinian refugee camps. Finally, overseas migration resulted in a mass exodus, in which one-third of the population were driven from the country and resettled in Canada, Australia, France, and the United States, as well as the Arab Gulf countries and beyond. The war migration, as noted above, led to demographic consequences, as Christian emigration was greater than Muslim emigration and consolidated the Maronite decline, while the aged and women were disproportionately left behind (Traboulsi 2012, 245). The central issue in the confessional division of political power in Lebanon, following the war, was the decline in the Maronite population and the need to readjust the power-sharing formula between Muslims and Christians.

THE SECOND REPUBLIC

After the 1989 Ta'if Agreement, which settled the civil war, Lebanon formed a "Second Republic" (Hage 2001). The power-sharing formula was revised, so that the overall ratio of Christian to Muslims in parliament was equal, with each allocated sixty-four seats (Traboulsi 2012, 107), while the power of the presidency was revised to be more ceremonial and the role of the prime minister was elevated to have more executive power.

Since the Spring Revolution of 2005, which saw the Syrian army withdraw from Lebanon and the July 2006 War with Israel, there has been an ongoing political struggle between the March 8 coalition and the March 14 coalition. On one side is the pro-Syria, Hezbollah; Shi'ite led March 8 alliance, which includes the Free Patriotic Movement and the Druze among others. On the other is the anti-Syria, Sunni-dominated March 14 alliance, dominated by the Future Movement, the LF, and the *Kataeb* Party. Lebanon almost returned to civil war in May 2008, but the 2008 Doha Agreement, which allocated Hezbollah the veto power in the Lebanese cabinet, ameliorated the conflict. The 2009 elections were won by the March 14 coalition, which subsequently took five months to form a national unity government. The Hezbollah-led opposition claimed they won 55 percent of the vote but were only allocated 45 percent of the seats in the cabinet (Al- Amin 2009). In the formation of the national unity government on November 9, 2009, the final division of power was based on a 15-10-5 structure, which granted the March 14 coalition fifteen ministers, the March 8 opposition ten, and President Michel Sleiman five seats, which guaranteed him the tipping vote (Sakr and Qawas 2009). It was not to last.

The tendency toward stalemates and deadlocks between the two opposing camps continued, with the Lebanese government caught in recurrent episodes of political paralysis, between two opposing political blocks after 2009 (Ofeish 1999). The Christian political parties and other minorities are effectively divided between the two major political blocks, leaving the division of power on a delicate knife-edge (Humphrey 2011).[5] The stalemate worsened after the Mikati government collapsed on March 22, 2013.[6] The new parliament, led by Prime Minister Salam, first extended its mandate for seventeen months, in May 31, 2013, and again on November 5, 2014, for an additional thirty-one months. Furthermore, Lebanon's opposing political blocks failed to elect a new president after forty-two failed attempts, following the departure of President Michel Suleiman on May 25, 2014, from the top Christian post.[7] After a two-and-a-half-year political vacuum, General Michel Aoun was elected as president on November 1, 2016, resolving the protracted political deadlock for the time being, after the outbreak of associated garbage, water, electricity, and security crises, which will be discussed further in chapter 5. This was the third such protracted crisis and collapse of the government since 2005 (The Daily Star 2013d). However, the newly formed national unity government soon fell into another political deadlock over the new electoral law for the election due in May 2017, with the two opposing political blocks divided between a proportional voting law and a 1960 "orthodox law" (Dakroub 2017), which critics argued would reinforce sectarian voting patterns (The Daily Star 2017). Ultimately, a new proportional voting law was implemented for the 2018 election.

While some analysts argued only external powers, such as Iran or Saudi Arabia, could resolve Lebanon's deadlock "from above," civil and women's rights activists called for a secular solution to Lebanon's confessional deadlock, which would reinvigorate civil society and women's rights in the country, as chapters 4, 5, and 6 examine. Others have argued Lebanon's problems are not sectarian, so much as political. The relationship between sects and sectarianism is a tautological one, which is ultimately reductive (Majed 2016). Political sectarianism exists but is not a homogenous unit of analysis; rather sects are the product of a political system, which divides power based on sect. For Weiss (2010, 14), sectarianism has been linked to the administration of Lebanon since the late Ottoman period and presents a chicken and egg argument: "which came first, sects or sectarianism?" Rather, he argues sects and sectarianism are dialectically intertwined. They emerge from specific cultural and social conditions, which produce political sectarianism, as a mode of social reproduction and identification, which limits the formation of national identities and reinforces patriarchal authority.

GENDERED CITIZENSHIP AND PATRIARCHAL KINSHIP

The mutually reinforcing relationship between the sectarian system and patriarchal control within the family has been a common finding made by scholars of Lebanese studies, which Joseph refers to as a system of patriarchal connectivity (Joseph 1999a, b). Joseph (1999a, 117) views the brother-sister relationship in Arab families as an extension of the father-daughter relationship, whereby the honor of the patrilineage depends upon the modesty of daughters. She suggests, however, it is the connectivity in the brother-sister relationship through which women learn that to be loved by a man is to be controlled by a man and the brother, conversely, learns that it is his role to control and regulate the sexuality of the women he loves (Joseph 1999a, 139–140). Humphrey (1998, 93), likewise, observes that the regulation of women is central to the construction of manliness in Lebanon: "In honor men's regulation of women is a measure of their social standing. According to men, social order requires them to assume responsibility for women to prevent social chaos."

While the secular critique of the sectarian structure of the Lebanese state was a key conflict during the Lebanese civil war, as noted earlier (Traboulsi 2012, 196), parallels are evident in the secular discourse of the contemporary Lebanese women's movement. This is because Lebanese citizenship is gendered (Joseph 2010, 12; Thompson 2000). Women do not have full nationality rights and cannot pass citizenship onto their children if they marry a non-Lebanese citizen. Traboulsi (2012, 110) argues that the Lebanese constitution is founded upon a fundamental dichotomy between the "judicial and political equality of all Lebanese as citizens (*muwatinin*)" and their institutional inequality as religious subjects (*ahlin*), belonging to a hierarchy of religious sects. However, the inequality of Lebanese (male) citizens/ subjects is built upon the fundamental inequality of women and their exclusion from full citizenship rights. Indeed, the gendered and sectarian-based construction of citizens is noted in the region more generally (Babst and Tellier 2012). As the next chapter examines further, Lebanon's fifteen[8] personal status codes for Catholics, Orthodox, Sunnis, Shi'ites, and Druze codify patrilineality in religious law and allocate women unequal marriage, divorce, custody and property rights (Mikdashi 2010; Joseph 2000, 130). That is, family law is located within religious law and, as Joseph (2010, 13) argues, it is "non-negotiable." Moreover, Joseph (2000, 21) theorizes that sectarian pluralism is underpinned by a kin-based patriarchal authority whereby:

> Social control has been achieved in Lebanon largely through the discipline of extended patriarchal kinship. I define patriarchy as the privileging of males and seniors (including women) and the rationalization of male and senior privilege in the idioms and moralities of kinship seen as organized along gendered and aged structures of authority legitimated by religious authority.

Secular citizenship, on the other hand, is posited upon an individual conception of the human citizen/subject, based upon a civil legal code and a secular state, whereby the particularistic ties of the family and religion are overcome (Joseph 2010, 13). The tension between religious authority, based upon differentiated personal status codes, citizenship rights, and women's rights has been at the heart of women's rights struggles in Lebanon since the French Mandate (Thompson 2000, 150). Therefore, the contemporary Lebanese women's movement recognizes that, in order to achieve gender equality and full citizenship rights, women and men need to transcend the dichotomy between citizenship and religion (*muwatinin* and *ahlin*).

THE REPRODUCTION OF SECT/NATION IN LEBANON

Lebanon is exceptional in the Middle Eastern region, due to what Weiss refers to as a unique form of sectarian modernity (Weiss 2010, 15). Consistent with the heterogeneous structure of the country, the classical system of Lebanese kinship had four main features, according to Gulick (1954, 297): village endogamy, devotion to land, religious orientation, and the predominance of kinship statuses. These four features of the social system of the Lebanese village maintained the distinctiveness of each sect (*ta'ifa*) and ensured that land (*ard*) was passed from one generation to the next, yet ownership was maintained within the patrilineage (*bayt*). The distinctive form of endogamous marriage across the sectarian groupings was *bint 'amm* marriage, also referred to as father's brother's daughter (FBD) marriage, between patrilateral parallel cousins.

For example, Kepler-Lewis (1968, 147–148) conducted a detailed ethnographic study of the Maronite Catholic village of Hadchit, in the late 1940s and found that the social structure of the village followed the broader sociopolitical pattern elsewhere in Lebanon. He estimated that 25 percent of marriages were contracted within the patrilineage (*bayt*), 99 percent of marriages were contracted within the village (*day'aa*), and 100 percent were contracted within the sect (*ta'ifa*). He found that marriage within the patrilineage was due to few marriageable women within a small village, at the time, and to the preference for in-group endogamy, which regulated the system of land tenure (the land-people relation), whereby the daughter's share of land was reincorporated back into the patrilineage. While much has changed in Lebanon since the ethnographic observations of Gulick and Kepler-Lewis in the 1950s, the institution of marriage has remained the subject of contestation in modern Lebanon. With internationalization and urbanization, along with rising levels of female education, as noted in the preface, social transformation has followed. The relationship between the sectarian social and political system and the institution of marriage is now the subject of national debate, as young people seek to push the boundaries of endogamous marriage (Mikdashi 2010; Hyndman-Rizk 2015), a topic we return to in chapter 6.

CONCLUSION

This chapter provided an overview of Lebanese history and the consistent role of religious difference in the governance of the polity since the

Mutasarrifate, under the Ottomans, through to the French Mandate and the formation of Lebanon as an independent nation-state in 1943. The central contradiction, as noted by Traboulsi (2012), is the dichotomy between citizenship status and religious affiliation. However, a lasting resolution to the contradiction is yet to be found, resulting in periods of crisis, war, and protracted deadlocks between the confessions since 1943. The machinations of the region have also played a role in Lebanon's travails. A third key element, which this chapter considered, which has been examined to a lesser extent in the historiographic literature, is the importance of the institution of marriage and women's relational citizenship rights for the reproduction of sectarian difference. The next chapter examines why Lebanon's plural personal status code system, which governs marriage, divorce, and all matters of personal status, is the lynchpin of women's inequality in Lebanon.

NOTES

1. The Druze are almost unique to Lebanon and are a sect within Shi'ite Islam, but their teachings also include reincarnation, which are thought to derive from connections to other Eastern religions and possibly to predate Islam and Christianity (Cobban 1985, 22).

2. For further information on Ottoman *millets* see: https://www.oxfordbibliographi es.com/view/document/obo-9780195390155/obo-9780195390155-0231.xml.

3. There has been no census in Lebanon since 1932 as it would substantiate that the Maronites no longer are the majority sect in Lebanon (Humphrey, 1998).

4. See *The Daily Star* for the number of Syrian refugees in Lebanon and region: http://www.dailystar.com.lb/News/Middle-East/2013/Oct-19/235073-unhcr-stres ses-need-to-offer-syrian-refugees-safe-harbor.ashx#axzz2iQKApMSQ.

5. Some would argue that only Hezbollah has the decisive military advantage, as it is the only militia, which retained its weapons after the civil war. Meanwhile, there has been no census since 1932.

6. See, *The Guardian*. "The Lebanese Government Collapse." Accessed March 22, 2013, www.theguardian.com.

7. See N. Malas, *Wall Street Journal*, May 25, 2014. http://online.wsj.com/news/ articles/SB10001424052702303749904579583032940250584.

8. See http://genderindex.org/country/lebanon.

Chapter 3

Gender and Personal Status Law in Lebanon

INTRODUCTION

This chapter examines Lebanon's complex system of legal pluralism and the evolution of the division between civil and religious law, dating back to the French Mandate. While the Ottomans developed the *millet* system, as noted in the previous chapter, whereby subjects of non-Muslim religious affiliations were governed in accordance with their faith, this mode of governing religious difference was codified into fifteen separate personal status codes for eighteen recognized religious confessions in Lebanon during the French Mandate (Hanf 2015, 3). This chapter examines how the personal status codes were developed into the system of family law, which operates in Lebanon today. The chapter starts by discussing the anthropology of marriage systems and the trend toward the democratization of personal relationships in marriage in late modernity. The chapter then examines the differences between the Christian and Muslim personal status codes and women's separate and unequal access to marriage, divorce, and child custody rights across all personal status codes.

MARRIAGE SYSTEMS AND WOMEN AS OBJECTS OF EXCHANGE

Marriage systems have long been the subject of scholarly inquiry, particularly in anthropology, due to the discipline's long-standing interest in the relationship between the system of marriage and the structure of kinship in different societies. While Radcliffe-Brown theorized that the biological family was the basic unit of kinship, Levi-Strauss thought otherwise and argued that "what confers upon kinship its sociocultural character is not what it retains from nature, but rather, the essential way in which it diverges from nature" (In Levi-Strauss 2000 [1963], 345). Levi-Strauss was more interested in the relationship between the universal structure of the human mind and the structure of kinship in different societies and drew on theoretical trends which had developed in structural linguistics (McGee and Warms 2000). In order to prove his hypothesis, that kinship systems operate through the simple or complex juxtaposition of elementary structures, Levi-Strauss built on the scholarship of Mauss (1967 [1925]), who studied extensively the role of reciprocity in human exchange systems, in his classic book *The Gift* (McGee and Warms 2000). In *The Elementary Structures of Kinship*, Levi-Strauss (1949) went on to argue, in contrast to Radcliffe-Brown, that "The basic unit of kinship . . . is actually a direct result of the universal presence of an incest taboo. That is really saying that in human society a man must obtain a woman from another man who gives him a daughter or a sister" (Levi-Strauss 2000 [1963], 342). Moreover, it is the relationship between brothers-in-law, which forms the "axis around which the kinship structure is built" (Levi-Strauss 2000 [1963], 342). In this formulation, women could be traded as wives, in either a circular or asymmetrical marriage system, whereby a human chain (of men) passed women in one direction and gifts in the opposite direction (Levi-Strauss 1949). Thus, for Levi-Strauss (1949, 65), women were the "the supreme gift." But, could the order of the sexes be reversed in a symmetrical structure involving sisters, their brothers, their brother's wife and daughters instead? True, this might be theoretically, but not empirically possible, according to Levi-Strauss, because "In human society, it is the men who exchange the women, and not vice versa" (Levi-Strauss 2000 [1963], 342).

Gregory (1982, 29–30) in *Gifts and Commodities* drew on Mauss, Levi-Strauss, and Marx (1967 [1867]) in his analysis of gift exchange systems and examined the circulation of both people and things in a dialectical relationship of production and consumption. Production, according to Gregory (1982, 33), is an "objectification process that converts people's labor energies into things, while consumption is a personification process which permits the survival of people." The exchange of women in marriage is the key conversion process, which links production and consumption into a structural whole (Gregory 1982, 33). The problem for women in this formulation, however, is their objectification and conversion into the "supreme" gift/thing for circulation in the system of exchange. By definition, slaves, like cattle according to Gregory (1982, 37), are always the "object of exchange, never the transactor." Thus, women are reified as objects of marriage, in anthropological theories of exchange, but has this always been the case?

In contrast, Engels (1902) argued that it was "the overturning of the mother right, or matrilineal descent, that led to the defeat of the female sex" and the creation of private property, which required heirs, and thus the rise of marriage systems based on patrilineal descent and monogamy. However, Lerner (1986) reversed this argument; drawing on the work of Levi-Strauss (1949), she found that it was the reification of women's reproductive capacity, through the exchange of women as gifts in marriage, which made private property possible. As the original appropriation, it inscribed in law the unequal nature of the marriage contract. Lerner (1986, 49) writes:

> In the process women were thought of as possessions, as things—they became reified, while men became the reifiers because they conquered and protected. Women's reproductive capacity is first recognized as a tribal resource, then, as ruling elites develop, it is acquired as the property of a particular kin group.

Pierre Bourdieu (1998, 42), likewise, argued in *Masculine Domination* that the fundamental law of the structure of the market for symbolic goods, which perpetuates the relation of male domination and female submission, is that "women are treated there as objects which circulate upwards." He asserts, moreover, that the principle of the inferiority and exclusion of women in the mythico-ritual system is based upon a dissymmetry in the relation of subject/object and agent/instrument, which is set up between men and women in the domain of symbolic exchanges and, ultimately, in the production and reproduction of symbolic capital. The central domain for the operation of symbolic exchanges is the matrimonial market, the foundation of the social order, and the role of women in this market as objects who contribute to the expansion of the symbolic capital held by men (Bourdieu 1998, 43). However, for Bourdieu (1998, viii), it is not so much that the relation of male domination and female submission is natural, but rather that it is de-historicized as natural and eternal. In order, therefore, for the relation of domination to be reversed and for women to become subjects, not objects of marriage, the role of cultural institutions, as a whole, should be re-historicized through the process of social critique.

Marriage markets are divided into those governed by the practice of exogamy and those governed by endogamy. Exogamous marriage outside of the group facilitates alliances and mixing between groups. Endogamous marriage, by contrast, reinforces marriage within the group and in stratified societies "helps maintain social, economic, and political distinctions and preserve differential access to culturally valued resources" (Kottak 1994, 223). Endogamy is less common and is practiced where property rights are maintained within the family (Kottak 1994, 226). Kottak (1994, 225) points to a subtle mechanism whereby marriage rules are enforced, through the perception of inescapability so that "endogamic groups would never consider doing anything else." When functioning effectively, therefore, marriage systems are perceived to be immutable and inevitable.

For Levi-Strauss (1949) the perpetuation of the system of sister exchange was built upon compulsory marriage rules. Salisbury (1956, 640) alternately referred to a system of "obligatory marriages rules," which guided the types of marriages contracted within a given society. While Levi-Strauss (1949) noted the universal incest taboo and exogamy, as being key to the exchange of women and gift exchange systems, this is not the case in the Middle Eastern region; rather it is the role of *endogamous unions*, within the lineage and sect, in the form of father's brother's daughter marriage, or *bint 'amm* marrriage, which transmitted patrilineal property rights and obligations between the generations (Moghadam 2004). If women were "exchanged," they were exchanged within the patrilineage and between brothers, first, and within the sect, second, a point to which we return, later in this chapter. Moreover, the rules of patrilineal descent transmit more than property; in Lebanon, as such, religious identity and citizenship, as a mode of production and reproduction (Godelier in Seymour-Smith 1986), are also transmitted through the rules of patrilineal descent, codified within the personal status codes of the Christian and Muslim confessions.

By contrast, the concept of romantic love and marriage are often represented as being in an irresolvable contradiction to one another cross culturally. Jankowiak and Paladino (2008, 2) write of sex, love, and companionship as forming a tripartite conundrum, which human societies struggle to overcome: "no matter how socially humane or politically enlightened, spiritually attuned, or technologically adapted, failure to integrate sex and love is the name of the game . . . dissatisfaction is everywhere." The arranged marriage, on the other hand, is the norm cross culturally, while romantic love is dismissed as an unruly inclination and a potentially subversive social force (Kottak 1994, 228). However, throughout the world the pursuit of romantic love is disrupting traditional marriage systems (Jankowiak and Paladino 2008), leading Kottak (1994, 225) to ask, "why something [love] so central to our [Western] culture has been so ignored?" The reason for the neglect, according to Kottak (1994, 228), is that falling in love is considered to be at odds with the traditional social institutions, which knit people together in an orderly fashion. By contrast, Doron (2012, 429) writes of the fusion of love and arranged marriage in modern India into the "love arranged marriage," whereby both individual desire and family responsibility can be met. In counterpoint, Bourdieu (1998, 108) proposes that women merely "learn to love the man, which social destiny assigned to them," their *amor fati*, whereby they unconsciously reproduce their own sublimation. However, the quest for love, and not "social destiny," is a potentially destabilizing social crisis in a marriage system and society based upon obligation, as Salisbury (1956, 640) termed.

For Giddens (1992, 2–3), the explanation for this puzzle is that a revolution is taking place within intimate relationships in modernity, as a result of the democratization of both personal relationships and society and the development of equality between the sexes. This transformation arises, he argues, out of the emergence of a post-traditional social order, whereby individual choice, not economic necessity, male privilege, or the traditional marriage contract determines the construction of the new pure relationship. However, Giddens (1992) concludes that the transformation in the realm of intimate relationships is deeply subversive to social institutions, as a whole, and is leading to a destabilization of the gender order and a male backlash against their loss of control over female sexuality. Likewise, the entry of women into the public sphere and the development of female economic independence are factors contributing to the destabilization of the gender order (Fowler 2003, 480–418), as will be evident in Lebanon's civil marriage debate, which will be examined in chapter 6.

THE CHANGING DYNAMICS OF
MARRIAGE IN THE MIDDLE EAST

"Marriage is universally looked upon as a trap. The women equate marriage with unending toil and burdens. They primarily resent the woman's role, which affords a wife, and especially a wife with children, no leisure . . . husbands share, but never to an equal degree, the endless trials and burdens . . . they are never thought of as partners or companions, only people trapped side by side in the same fix" (Williams 1958, 232). This quote written by the ethnographer Williams (1958), who undertook extensive field research in Lebanon after the Second World War, examining stability and change in village life. Focusing on the Maronite Catholic village of Hadchit, he reflects on the perceived nature of married life in the village during the 1950s. He depicts marriage is a "trap" for women, more than men, a source of "endless trials and burdens" and agency deprivation. This sentiment, more broadly, is the core of changing dynamics of marriage since the 1950s in the Middle Eastern region and Lebanon. The key dynamics of change focused on the role of personal autonomy and change over continuity in relation to the nature of the marriage contract. Broadly, this process of change has three key characteristics: the democratization of relationships within marriage, the preference for women's equality and agency, whereby their choice and consent are recognized in the selection of marriage partners, hence a decline in the practice of arranged marriages. These changes to the institution of marriage can be seen in the demands from women's rights movements to reform the systems of family law, accordingly, and the nature of the marriage contract.

The changing dynamics of marriage have been noted across the Middle Eastern region. Much research has been written on the changing marriage

dynamics underway across many societies in the Middle East, from Saudi
Arabia, to Egypt and Syria (Cuno 2015; Al-Rasheed 2013; Thompson 2000;
Joseph 1996). Thompson (2000) discusses the beginning of the changing
conversation on women's role in marriage and society, during the French
Mandate, and a critique put forward by *Zayn al-Din*, that the Islamic message
generally favored equal rights between men and women and that the specific
privileges granted in the *Qur'an* to a man over his wife and sisters, such as
in inheritance, should not justify a universal superiority of men over women
(Thompson 2000, 126). While Al Din called for unveiling and free interpretation of the *Qur'an*, her arguments were quickly rejected by the ulama
and the principle of paternalism upheld in family law and religious authority
(Thompson 2000, 134). Moreover, Thompson argues that paternalism and
gender hierarchy were central to the colonial administration of Lebanon
(Thompson 2000, 3–4).

Charrad (2001, 28–29) notes that in Islamic law, the *Shari'a*, there is no
separation between religious and secular law, the "sacred and civil are one
and the same thing." Moreover, laws regulating social life are integral to the
Islamic religion itself; thus, being a Muslim implies accepting a system of
jurisprudence and way of life (Charrad 2001, 29). The field of kinship and
family life includes the most explicit recommendation and specific principles
covering personal status, family life, and relations among kin and property
rights (Charrad 2001, 29). These are drawn from several core religious texts,
which constitute the *Shari'a*, including *Qur'an*, *Sunna*, or model of behavior,
as recorded in the pronouncements of the Prophet Muhammad, the *Hadith*,
qiyas, and *ijma*, the foundation and consensus of legal reasoning, as part of
fiqh, Islamic jurisprudence (Charrad 2001, 30). Within the dominant Sunni
tradition of Islam, there are four different schools of legal thought, which
reflect how Islam mingled with local traditions in different parts of the world.
Each tradition has some noteworthy variations pertaining to women, kinship, and family. The four schools, or rites, are Hanafi, Malaki, Shafi'i, and
Hanbali (Charrad 2001, 31). Two schools are dominant within Shi'ite Islam,
the Ja'fari and Zaidi schools. Each has slightly different rulings regarding
marriage contracts and different schools of legal thought are more prevalent
in different regions of the Middle East. In North Africa the Malaki school is
more dominant, in Lebanon the Hanafi and Ja'fari schools are more common
for Sunni and Shi'ite Islamic personal status codes, respectively (Human
Rights Watch 2015). The enduring orientation of kinship relations within
Islamic family law, Charrad (2001) notes, is governed by two key principles:
the control of women by male relatives and the favoring of the cohesiveness
of the patrilineage over the conjugal family unit (Charrad 2001, 31). These
principles are reflected in the fragility of the marriage bond, as expressed
through the laws on divorce and polygamy and the separation of marital

property (Charrad 2001, 31), with each spouse retaining control over his/her own property, as it does not become part of the common conjugal patrimony (32). Thus, marriage is, above all, a contract between families, while "the patrilineage occupies a privileged position" (Charrad 2001, 32).

By contrast, Cuno (2015) examines the emergence of the conjugal family as part of modernization discourses in Egypt. The shift to the conjugal family privileges the "nuclear family unit" over the extended patrilineal family, which was favored by Islamic family law, as noted by Charrad (2001). As the prevalence of polygyny declined among the upper classes, he argues, the conjugal family became part of nineteenth-century "civilizational" projects, based on the European enlightenment (Cuno 2015, 6–7). He notes that the average age of marriage increased, the architectural style of family homes changed, and the legal underpinning for marriage, based on the *Shari'a*, underwent a process of codification by the state, which was more rigid in the colonial and postcolonial context (Cuno 2015, 7).

Yet, Lerner (1986) notes, the principle of patriarchy in marriage, as enshrined in Islamic family law, predates both Islam and Christianity. It can be traced back to the ancient states of the Middle East, based on the family law principles set out in the Code Hammurabi and the Mesopotamian law, which eventually became part of Biblical law and later, Islamic family law. For example, Lerner (1986, 102) shows that "Babylonian and Assyrian law does show considerable parallels." Moreover, she concludes that the Assyrian laws are amendments to the Hammurabic law and the Hebrew law and half of the laws of the Covenant are parallel to the Hammurabic law (Lerner 1986, 102). Of the 282 laws of the Code of Hammurabi, 73 covered marriage and sexual matters and women are more restricted than men (Lerner 1986, 102), which assumed a fixed body of accepted norms for moral and social behavior. The social conditions of Mesopotamian women reflected a patriarchal society, which featured "patrilineal descent, property laws guaranteeing the inheritance rights of sons, male dominance in property and sexual relations, military, political and religious bureaucracies. These institutions were supported by patriarchal family and in turn constantly created by it" (Lerner 1986, 106). The principle of the bride price derives from Mesopotamian law, with the value of daughters reflected in their bride price, which could be used toward paying the bride price for a son's wedding. Bride price developed from bride purchase but gave certain rights of property and maintenance to married women. Likewise, the concept of marriage as a contract derived from the Hammurabi Code (Lerner 1986, 107), wherein women were allowed certain property rights. Unequal divorce rights between men and women existed in the Mesopotamian law, with men able to exercise their right to divorce through a public declaration, and by returning the dowry and half his property to the wife. Yet, for women they had to prove adultery and no fault.

Overall, Lerner (1986, 115) surmises that "This double standard is carried forward in Hebrew law, which allowed a husband to divorce his wife at will, but denied a woman the right to seek a divorce under any circumstances."

Leila Ahmed (1992), similarly, traces the continuity between the cultures of the ancient and modern Middle East. She notes that

> During the first Christian centuries the notion of women's seclusion, together with veiling and attitudes about the proper invisibility of women, became features of upper class life . . . they represented a coalescence of similar attitudes and practices originating within the various patriarchal cultures of the region. Mesopotamian, Persian, Hellenic, Christian and eventually Islamic cultures each contributed practices that both controlled and diminished women, and each also apparently borrowed the controlling and reductive practices of their neighbors. (Ahmed 1992, 18)

Moghadam (2004, 142) also notes that "like Judaism and Christianity before it, Islam came into being in a patriarchal society." Thus, endogamy, marriage within the lineage, and patrilineal descent were the key to the political and economic interests of men, which became codified in the ancient laws of the Middle East (Moghadam 2004). Nevertheless, Islamic family law introduced reforms that provided women with certain legal rights absent in Judaism and Christianity, according to Moghadam (Moghadam 2004, 142). These included a ban on female infanticide, a provision for women to be able to contract their own marriage, under certain conditions, receive and retain the bride price, retain control of wealth, as well as their inheritance, and receive maintenance. Yet, this was counterbalanced by limited maternal custody, with the patrilineage retaining child custody at varying ages for males and females, polygyny, unilateral male divorce, and unequal inheritance rights between men and women. Moreover, what rights women gained could be circumvented by more powerful male relatives (Moghadam 2004, 142). As the family law became codified and modernized across the Muslim world in the postcolonial states of the Middle East, they were based on a combination of Islamic, Swiss, French, and Belgian legal systems, a point we return to in the next section.

When considering the evolution of patriarchal cultural and legal systems, Kandiyoti (1988, 278) writes of a patriarchy belt in North Africa, the Muslim Middle East, South Asia, and East Asia, specifically India and China. She notes that the key to reproduction under classical patriarchy is the patrilocal extended household, the control of senior men over women and junior men, and the transition from kin-based to tributary modes of production. This is also referred to in the anthropological literature as the patrilineal virilocal complex, which involves the subordination and control of women and it cuts across cultural and religious boundaries, including between Hinduism,

Confucianism, and Islam (Kandiyoti 1988). Thus, a continuity can be found between marriage systems. Moreover, in classic patriarchy women do not have a claim on the father's patrimony, whether the system is based on dowry or bride price, both women's labor and their offspring are appropriated by the patrilineage (Kandiyoti 1992, 279). Women must seek patriarchal bargains, or loopholes, to exercise agency and power, usually in the role of mother-in-law.

POSTCOLONIAL STATES, PLURAL RELIGIOUS FAMILY LAW, AND GENDER EQUALITY

The systems of family law prevalent in the Middle East, following with the formation of the postcolonial states, saw the institutionalization of legal dualism, with a separation between the jurisdiction of religious and civil law and the location of family law within religious law and its codification into plural personal status codes, as in the case of Lebanon. In all states in the Middle East, Islamic *Shari'a* law, to a lesser or greater extent, influenced the formation of the modern family law system that developed, except for Turkey and Tunisia, which adopted a secular family law system, based on a civil code, at the time of independence (Moghadam 2004). During the 1950s in Tunisia, under the *Bourguiba* reforms, polygamy and unilateral male divorce were abolished, while Turkey adopted a civil code from Switzerland in 1926 under Kemal Ataturk (Moghadam 2004, 146). Morocco reformed their family law in 2004, the *Moudawana*, to improve women's equality in divorce, the minimum age of marriage, and maternal child custody, after an extended period of national debate (Foblets 2016; Zoglin 2009). Meanwhile, Jordan, Saudi Arabia, and Iran have family laws, which are extremely controlling of women, based on the most patriarchal interpretations of Islamic law, which has affected the legal status of women and girls (Moghadam 2004).

In the case of Iran, during the Pahlavi period, the Family Protection Act of 1967 and 1973 gave women more rights in family matters and raised the legal age of marriage. Nasserist Egypt also implemented reforms to the family law, but retained male privilege. However, in the 1970s and 1980s as Islamists gained in power, many of those reforms have been reversed, with revised family laws implemented in Algeria, Egypt, and Iran. Saudi Arabia remains the most conservative kingdom in the Middle East, with its male guardianship system, which requires fathers, husbands, and sons to be a legal guardian, referred to as a *Wali*, for daughters, sisters, and wives, making women into legal minors for their whole lives.

Rasheed (2013, 16) attributes religious state nationalism in Saudi Arabia, under the influence of the *Wahhabist* interpretation of Islam, to the persistence of male guardianship,[1] which includes gender segregation in workplaces and education, and male permission for travel, healthcare, and release from prison. While women gained the right to drive in 2018, and legal reforms have allowed women to have limited participation in the *Shura* Council since 2013, liberalizing the fields women can work in, they also no longer require a guardian's permission to work (Watch 2016). Nonetheless, public media attention has been drawn to the system 2018 and 2019, when several prominent Saudi women escaped their legal guardians and sought asylum in Australia, Canada, and elsewhere.[2] Whether under secular nationalism or religious nationalism, personal status codes and family law have formed the core mechanism by which Middle Eastern states have controlled women's lives and reinforced private patriarchy, or developed integrated forms of state patriarchy, for which women are boundary markers (Al-Rasheed 2013, 16):

> Like secular nationalism, *Wahhabi* religious nationalism seeks to preserve the family and women's status within the private domain in order to achieve the ultimate restoration of the pious religious community. Women become boundary markers that visibly and structurally distinguish the pious nation from other ungodly polities. (16)

The link between women as symbols of nations and subnational sects is a common motif across the region, but according to Joseph (1996a), is the key to understanding the relationship between citizenship, nation, and family law in the Middle East, wherein a contradiction arises between their roles as mothers in families and reproducers of sects and nations. As such, Moghadam argues modern Middle Eastern ideals of the role of women and family are striking in their agreement that marriage and family are "central to social reproduction and are the sublime manifestation of Divine Will and Purpose" (Moghadam 2004, 138). With social and political change accelerating across the region, three key trends can be discerned. First, the erosion of the patriarchal extended household, second, socioeconomic development and the increase in women's educational attainment, and third, middle-class social movements with a moral discourse emphasizing traditional family values. Thus, protecting and reforming personal status codes have been key to debates on women's roles in society and the role of the family in Middle Eastern societies and the future of the nation, with the dissolution of the traditional family (Moghadam 2004, 138).

THE ORIGINS OF LEBANON'S FAMILY LAW

While there are differences and similarities between Muslim and Christian personal status codes, women are effectively divided between the personal status codes and unequal in all of them, particularly with respect to maternal custody and divorce law. In Lebanon, all matters of personal status are the preserve of the relevant personal status code of Lebanon's eighteen recognized religious communities and fifteen religious courts servicing Muslims, Christians, and Jews. Within the Muslim personal status codes there are separate religious courts for Sunni's, Shi'ites, Druze, Alawites, which we will examine further later in the chapter. Within the Christian personal status codes there are separate religious courts for Catholics, Orthodox, Protestants, Coptic, and Armenian Catholic and Orthodox communities. There is also a separate religious court for Jews, although Lebanon's Jewish community is very small, since the formation of Israel after 1948, to where most subsequently emigrated. Each religious court has a presiding judge (*qadi*), with limited or no state oversight. All of Lebanon's personal status codes were supposedly codified by the state, but the Sunni code has never been formally codified by the state (Human Rights Watch 2015). The system is not unique in the Middle East, as noted earlier, as most family law systems in Middle Eastern countries are based on Islamic *Shari'a* law, or the Ottoman Law of Family Rights of 1917 (Moghadam 2004, 146).

As Thompson (2000) notes, the dual positioning of women in a gendered and colonial hierarchy was central to Mandate Lebanon, when the system of legal pluralism, practiced in Lebanon today, developed and relegated the control of women to subnational communities, or sects, in a complex system of legal pluralism, which underpins the reproduction of the consociational political system as a whole. As Max Weiss aptly writes, "the preservation of the personal status laws are part and parcel of the sectarian representation of the political system" (Weiss 2010, 123). Women are both the subject and object of religious family laws, whereby both sect and citizen are reproduced through the institution of marriage. But are Lebanon's personal status codes unique to the postcolonial state, or are they a continuation of the system of family law prevalent in the French colonial and Ottoman periods?

One view is that Lebanon's system of family law derives from the Ottoman period, where it was the practice, under the *millet* system, for each religious minority, or non-Muslim community within the empire, to maintain their own personal status law. While Weiss (2010, 99) argues Lebanon's legal framework, as it developed during the French Mandate, "was not neatly transposed from the *millet* system, to be sure, the institutions of Lebanese sectarianism appear to be derivative of the *millet* system in some way." With independence, sectarian difference became institutionalized within the Lebanese polity. While the religion of state for the Ottoman Empire was Islam and Islamic law was the official law of the empire, the "People of the book, Christians and Jews," were recognized as *dhimmis*, as noted in chapter 2, and entitled to maintain their own personal status law under Ottoman rule (Hanf 2015). Yet, the Ottoman's modernized family law with the introduction of the Family Law Act in 1917, which, in some instances, offered more rights to women than those that were later codified under the personal status codes institutionalized in Lebanon after independence (Shehadeh 1998). For instance, under the Ottoman family law, women can stipulate in the *niqa*, the marriage contract, to forbid the husband to take a second wife or stipulate that if their husband takes a second wife the first or second wife will be divorced automatically (Shehadeh 1998, 505).

The Lebanese legal system which developed during the French Mandate, and following independence in 1943, according to Thompson (2000), is a dual legal system, whereby civil and criminal law are separated from religious family law. Moreover, it was a hybrid of French republican law, in which civil law dominates, and family law was left to the autonomy of religious courts for each confession under the adjudication of the relevant personal status code. In the 1920s the French attempted to introduce a civil law 60 LR to family law matters; however, it was never implemented, a point to which we return in chapter 6. Moreover, under the National Pact, Lebanon's consociational system attributes seats in parliament based on sect, as noted in chapter 2, so that the logic of perpetuating sectarian difference lies at the heart of the confessional system. Separate personal status laws, for each recognized religious community, were considered a core component of the National Pact, by allowing each religious community autonomy to follow the laws of their religion, in all matters of personal status including marriage, divorce, inheritance, property, and child custody.

In the case of Lebanon, multiple attempts have been made since the 1930s to reform the system of plural personal status law and harmonize women's rights across the codes, as well as to introduce a unified personal status code. To date no significant law reform has succeeded, as religious leaders guard jealously their autonomy and control of family law matters. It has been noted, that the core struggle of the women's movement of the 1920s was the establishment of women's political rights, while the key struggle of the 1930s was the establishment of social and legal reform (Thompson 2000). In both cases, the struggles were deferred, with women's voting rights not included in the 1926 Constitution. In the case of women's suffrage, the right to vote was eventually achieved in 1952, following the foundation of the Lebanese Republic in 1943, although the 1936 constitution included no provision for women's voting rights (Thompson 2000, 147). Yet, family law remains unreformed, with the parallel legal system an enduring feature of the Lebanese political and legal system (Thompson 2000, 149).

Following the retreat of the Ottomans, the Lebanese religious leaders, in conjunction with support from nationalist leaders, who opposed French rule, sought to reestablish the Ottoman *millet* system, through the establishment of separate religious courts in the 1930s for each religious community. In 1935, a petition was put before the French Mandate to introduce "uniform marriage laws," which would include a single minimum age of marriage. In 1936, the French Mandate issued a decree reaffirming the autonomy of personal status law, but Muslim resistance resulted in a revised decree in 1938. However, the French, under Gabriel Puaux, with support of the Maronite Catholic community, introduced a revised law to "regulate, on a civil level, the conflicts among religious laws and to permit a unified national life based on the essential equality of personal rights" (Thompson 2000, 152). The law also required civil law to be followed in nonfamily law matters and marriages to be registered with the state. Massive resistance to the new law followed, particularly from Muslim communities, and Puaux concluded that "all reform of personal status law was doomed to failure" and publicly retracted the decree by national radio broadcast (Thompson 2000). There has been no successful reform or harmonization of Lebanon's personal status law system ever since.

While there are commonalities between the different codes, there are also important differences and women have differential rights under all of Lebanon's personal status laws. Overall, it is argued, that while the Lebanese constitution does not discriminate between the sexes, the law does at different levels, most particularly in relation to married women. Thus, Shehadeh (1998, 502) concludes that "One is left with the impression that upon marriage, a Lebanese woman forfeits most of her rights as an individual and citizen." Moreover, women are relegated to second-class status in civil law once they are married and, effectively become "wards of their husbands." The intersection between personal status law and civil law forms the knot, which mutually reinforces women's unequal legal status and relational rights. Hence, the marriage is, above all, a contract between unequal parties, which is guaranteed by law (Shehadeh 1998, 503).

THE CONSTITUTION AND PERSONAL STATUS CODES

The legislative framework governing Lebanon's system of legal pluralism, in matters of personal status, has three components. First, the Lebanese constitution recognizes the equality of all Lebanese citizens and the principle of non-discrimination (Geagea et al. 2014). Additionally, the Lebanese constitution guarantees in the preamble the absolute freedom of belief, while in Article 9, it guarantees the respect for the "personal status law of the population, of whatever religious sect they belong" (Geagea et al. 2014, 2). The core text, which underpins the system of family law is the 1936 Law: Resolution no.60LR. As noted by Thompson (2000) earlier, this law was enacted during the French Mandate, but did not make membership of a sect mandatory, but rather provided a provision for every Lebanese to regulate their personal status, in accordance with civil law, not personal status law. However, as noted earlier, due to resistance to the adoption of a civil code, it was not enacted. The law issued on April 2, 1951, in Article 33, asked all Christian and Jewish sects to submit their personal status law and code of procedure for the religious courts to the state for approval, and the government has yet to codify them; thus, the courts continue to follow their own customs (Geagea et al. 2014). In addition to the personal status laws, the Christian sects follow the laws of the Bible, the apostles, general and national Synods, and decrees issued by the Maronite Patriarchs, as well as to foreign supreme courts, such as the Rota Roman Catholic Church (Geagea et al. 2014). For the Christian sects, Catholic and Orthodox, the following laws regulate personal status matters (Human Rights Watch 2015), see table 3.1:

Table 3.1 Christian Personal Status Codes and Sources of Law

Christian Sects	Code Followed
The Catholic communities (Maronite, Melkite, Armenian, Syriac, Roman, and Chaldean)	Sacrament of Marriage in the Eastern Church, February 23, 1949, The Eastern Catholic Church, October 18, 1990, New Western Civil Code, January 25, 1990.
The Greek Orthodox communities	Code of Procedure of the Greek Orthodox Patriarchate of Antioch and All the East, October 16, 2003, and Code of Civil Procedure.
The Armenian Orthodox Communities	Code of Procedure and personal status law for the Armenia Orthodox sect, issued February 22, 1949.
The Syriac Orthodox communities	Personal status law of the Syriac Orthodox sect, issued February 22, 1949.
The Assyrian Eastern Orthodox communities	Personal status law for the Assyrian Eastern Orthodox sect, issued February 22, 1949.
The Coptic Orthodox communities (Nestorian)	In accordance with the personal status law of the Coptic Orthodox sect, issued September 11, 2010, or the Code of Civil Procedure regarding matters neither stipulated by nor conflicting with the 2010 law, or the Lebanese law of 1951 on powers of sects, or customs relative to the sect.
Evangelist/protestant communities	Personal status law of the Evangelist sect of Syria and Lebanon, April 1, 2005, and the civil laws in force.

The following codes apply for the governance of personal status matters for Muslim sects in Lebanon. As the Muslim community objected to the law 60LR, they never submitted their laws for ratification by the Lebanese parliament and a law of exemption for Muslims was enacted on 1939, Decree 53 (Human Rights Watch 2015), see table 3.2.

Table 3.2   Muslim Personal Status Codes

Muslim Sects	Code Followed
Sunni	The law governing the Sunni and Ja'afari *Shari'a* courts issued 16/7/1962 and the supreme Islamic court. Judgment No. 46, Family Judgments, issued in 2011, raised the age of child custody to twelve for boys and girls. Other sources are the Ottoman Law of Family Rights and the Imam Abu Hanifa school of law.
Shi'ite	Judge issues judgments in accordance with the Ja'afari school and personal status law of the Druze sect, issued 24/4/1948. May also refer to the Hanafi school of Islamic law. Not codified.
Druze	The law governing Druze courts, 9/3/1960.

The Role of Religious Courts and Judges

The religious courts have a great degree of autonomy to make their rulings in accordance with the personal status code of the relevant religious confession. There is little oversight by state judicial bodies of their rulings. The qualification of religious judges varies according to the confession and does not require a national law degree. Women are excluded from the role of judge in all confessions, except for the Evangelical and Armenian Orthodox confessions. There is also a lack of oversight by an independent tribunal, as specified in Article 14 of the International Covenant on Civil and Political Rights. Individuals who marry under a civil code will have their personal status matters heard by a civil court, following the laws of the country in which they married, which is applied, as will be discussed in chapter 6 on civil marriage reform. However, couples who hold a religious ceremony, in addition to a civil ceremony abroad, will be subject to religious laws and courts in Lebanon if there is a dispute, or a divorce. Furthermore, if the couple is Sunni, Druze, or Shi'ite, the religious court of each confession will not recognize their civil marriage and will apply their own religious laws if either spouse seeks their adjudication. Although Islamic courts receive state funding, and have done so since Ottoman times, there is little state oversight (Human Rights Watch 2015, 28–29).

Christian courts are independent of the state and receive no state funding. There is a first instance court for every Catholic Diocese in Lebanon and there is a collegiate tribunal for each Catholic confession, which hears personal status matters and annulments. The Roman Rota Court in the Vatican is the second-highest Catholic court and appeals go before the Supreme Tribunal of the apostolic Signature. The Orthodox confessions have first instance courts, presided over by one judge, or a chief judge and two member judges, depending on the confession. There is an Appellate court for each Orthodox confession. There is no mechanism to appeal the rulings of the Appellate court (Human Rights Watch 2015, 29–30).

In total, there are nineteen Sunni courts and twenty Ja'fari courts that rule on personal status matters in Lebanon. The first instance courts have individual judges. There is also a Supreme Islamic Court and a Supreme Ja'fari Court. There are six Druze courts and a Supreme Appellate Court, presided over by two judges and a chief judge in Beirut. The Lebanese Court of Cessation is Lebanon's highest court and the final arbiter of disputes, including examining the compatibility of religious codes and public order (Human Rights Watch 2015, 36). The court generally limits its ruling in relation to religious rules, but recently has intervened in child custody matters, which are more typically dealt with in religious courts (see section on Limited Maternal Child Custody below).

Judges are appointed with discretion by the spiritual authorities within each confession. However, some judges combine their judicial and clerical duties, but patriarchs and Bishops can appoint members of the judicial corps, as well as aids. Sunni and Ja'fari judges are appointed by the Supreme Islamic Authority, the cabinet, and the Islamic Judiciary Council. Druze judges are appointed by the recommendation of the minister of justice after consultation with the Initiates Council. There are also issues regarding barriers to accessing religious courts, due to the absence of legal aid and the high costs, particularly in the Christian courts, which are completely independent of the state and can set their own fees. Lawyers also do not have a minimum professional requirement to work before the religious courts. In the Catholic courts, they require a Catholic canon law license, but not a law license. Under the Islamic courts, Shi'ite and Sunni, a male relative can represent a woman in the court, without a law degree (Human Rights Watch 2015, 37–39).

Marriage and Divorce

Marriage is a bilateral contract, concluded in public whereby a couple agrees to live together for the sake of procreation. Marriage is conceived as a holy sacrament for the Christian sects, except for Protestants, while for the Muslim sects it is practiced as a conditional contract, while for the Jewish code it is a sanctification of both man and woman. Christian sects do not permit any conditions for the marriage, except for the *maher* or dowry; under Article 83 Catholics refuse conditional marriage, rather it is absolute. Sunni and Shi'ite personal status laws allow for conditional marriage, such as those stipulated in the *niqa*, giving the wife the right to divorce. The age of marriage varies between sects, with puberty for the Ja'fari code, twelve years for the Jewish law, seventeen and eighteen years for the remaining codes. With court intervention girls can be married at a younger age, from birth for the Jewish code, nine years for the Ja'fari law and ages thirteen to fifteen for the rest of the codes. While consent is required by all religious sects, it is in effect deferred when they are married as minors, as is permissible under all the codes (Shehadeh 1998, 504–505). Increasing the minimum age of marriage to eighteen is a key demand of the Lebanese women's movement, as will be discussed in chapters 4 to 6.

The payment of the *maher* finalizes the marriage in all sects. If the payment is paid from the husband to the wife it is a bride price. If the wife's family makes the payment to the husband's family, in the form of trousseau or immovable property, it is referred to as a dowry, or *ba'ina*. The former is practiced by Muslim family law and the latter by some Christians. Although sometimes Muslims will include both, while the *maher* is optional for Catholic sects (Shehadeh 1998). It is common practice for Muslim sects that half of the *maher* is paid upon marriage and the remainder upon repudiation, divorce, or widowhood. In either case, the bride is bought or sold and the marriage is a written agreement, which is witnessed. In the Orthodox sect, the *maher* becomes the wife's property after marriage. In the Muslim sects, the contract does not require a *sheikh* to be a witness, but a learned person is sufficient as witness to the contract, while the Christian codes require a priest to perform the wedding ceremony, which is a sacrament.

Access to divorce is unequally distributed between men and women and between personal status codes in Lebanon. Within the Islamic personal status codes men have a unilateral right to divorce, while women have a conditional right to divorce. The marriage is based upon a contract, *niqa*, and a bride price, *maher*, is paid to the bride and retained as a surety, as noted earlier, against the male right to unilateral divorce or repudiation, referred to as *talaq*. Men can pronounce divorce without cause, outside of any judicial proceeding. However, divorces that are not filed in the religious court are not recorded or enforced by the personal status department of the ministry of the interior. Hence, there is no binding court decision to oblige men to pay the deferred *maher*, or maintenance during the three-month waiting period, the *'idda* (which is three menstrual cycles) (Human Rights Watch 2015, 41). In Lebanon Sunnis follow the Hanafi law, which accepts that the pronouncements of divorce can be conditional, contingent, or qualified, including in the future (Shehadeh 1998). As long as the husband is of sound mind, he is unencumbered, he can pronounce divorce without the wife's presence. It can be revocable if during the waiting period, the *'idda*, a reconciliation is made and cohabitation resumes, in which case the divorce is revoked. The divorce is irrevocable, however, if the pronouncement is made three times consecutively. The so-called *talaq-e-biddat*, or instant divorce, is debatable as to its legality. It is not recognized by Shi'ite schools of law and some Sunni schools of law view the single and triple *talaq* as being much the same, as the waiting period must still be observed. If there is no reconciliation within the waiting period, the divorce is irrevocable. Still others insist on a waiting period of one month between pronouncements (Ghabour 2010–2017, 361). The divorce is effective after the waiting period and the husband is obliged to lodge the divorce in the *Shari'a* court[3] (Shehadeh 1998). As noted earlier, the Ottoman Family Law permitted women to be granted a divorce if a clause is stipulated in the *niqa* forbidding the husband from taking a second wife.

Overall, women appearing before Sunni, Shi'ite, and Druze courts are better able to end their marriages than women from Christian confessions are, but there is still discrimination. Women under Sunni and Druze personal status law are able to claim severance lawsuits, while under the Ja'fari personal status law, women are only able to initiate divorce if it is stipulated in the marriage contract, in which case they forfeit some or all of their financial rights, referred to as quittance. Yet, Sunni and Shi'ite confessions both limit the ability of women to end their marriages. Women can divorce if there is an *isma*, or a clause, within the Sunni marriage contract, stating that husband and wife have an equal right to initiate divorce, while Shi'ite women have an equivalent right. In effect, under the *isma*, women can divorce themselves. Women can also be delegated the right to divorce, *talaq al-tafwid*. Sunni women can also have an exclusive right to divorce, through the provision within the *isma* (Human Rights Watch 2015, 42). While the inclusion of an *isma*, within the marriage contract is permissible, it is not common in a society, which supports the male prerogative in this domain.

Severance refers to the dissolution of a marriage by religious judicial order, following request from either spouse, under specific conditions enumerated in the law. The Ja'fari courts do not recognize severance. In the case of severance, the marriage is terminated via quittance, or *khul* (mutual divorce) in which the wife forfeits her legal rights to the *maher* and spousal maintenance. *Khul* can also involve a payment of a sum to the husband to be granted a divorce without grounds stipulated in the law. Thus, marriage contract is confirmed as a business contract, in which the woman has to buy her freedom (Shehadeh 1998, 508). Both Sunni and Ja'fari courts recognize *khul*. However, Shi'ite women can terminate their marriages through sovereign divorce, via an order from a Shi'ite religious authority, which must be certified by the court (Human Rights Watch 2015, 42–43). The conditions for severance, under the Sunni and Druze personal status law, include unpaid spousal maintenance, impotence, contagious disease or insanity, on the part of the husband, a prolonged absence on the part of the husband, or if the husband commits adultery, under the Druze code. Hardship and discord are also grounds and twelve months is the waiting period.

Access to divorce under the Christian personal status codes is more limited, if not impossible. While women have a limited right to terminate their marriages, men can circumvent the restrictions imposed by the Christian personal status codes. The Catholic sects believe in the indissolubility of marriage, with separation, or separation de corps, only being recognized, in which case the couple live separately but remain married. Annulment will be granted under specific circumstances, such as a lack of consummation of the marriage, abandonment, or mental incapacity. The provisions vary between Catholics, Orthodox, and Protestant sects as to the conditions for annulment. There are instances when men have more provisions to claim for divorce than women, such as the wife not being a virgin on the wedding night, under the Orthodox personal status law. Overall, two aspects disproportionately affect women, first, spousal violence is not sufficient to prompt an end to a marriage, particularly under the Catholic codes, where mental incapacity is the only grounds that must exist prior to the marriage, which renders the husband incapable of assuming marital duties. Second, Christian men in Lebanon have the additional option of converting to Islam and remarrying without ever divorcing their Christian wives. There is no equivalent option for Christian women to bypass their personal status code through conversion, after their marriage has been consummated (Zalzal 1997).

Limited Maternal Child Custody

Across Lebanon's personal status codes, women do not retain the custody of children after divorce. As Shehadeh (2010, 219) notes, women's authority over children is delegated by their husbands, who have tutelage and guardianship over children in all matters spiritual and economic. To this end, women cannot provide passports, travel abroad with children, or open bank accounts for them, without their husband's approval. Women can lose rights to care for their children if they are found to have converted to another religion, been disobedient, or remarried. In the event of divorce or death of the husband, guardianship is awarded to the patrilineage, while the period of maternal custody is limited in all personal status codes. Under the Catholic code, if the husband dies abroad, guardianship is automatically transferred to the paternal grandfather, brother, and or cousin, before the mother (Shehadeh 2010, 219). The period of maternal custody ends at age two for boys and girls under the Catholic code, in the event of annulment or separation. For the Greek Orthodox code the period of maternal custody ends when boys are eleven and girls are thirteen, for the Protestant sect maternal custody ends when boys and girls are aged twelve and seven, respectively, and nine for the Armenian Orthodox, Assyrian, and Syriac Orthodox confessions. The period of maternal custody under the Muslim personal status codes ends at age twelve for boys and girls under the Sunni code, two and seven under the Shi'ite code, and seven and nine for boys and girls, respectively, under the Druze code. The key guiding principle is the absolute right of paternal guardianship and the limited period of maternal custody of young children. Hence, the children's age determines their residency, not their best interest. After the period of maternal custody ends, women may have limited visitation rights to their children and maintenance support ends. Women may also forfeit their child custody rights in a divorce agreement and the period of maternal custody can be cut short, if the husband claims unfitness or remarriage, or if the mother is from a different religion from the child, as children follow their father's religion. Thus, maternal custody rights are time-bound, conditional, and revocable, while male guardianship is absolute. Combined with the difficulties in accessing divorce and receiving maintenance, there are strong social and legal sanctions against women, which deter them from leaving a violent or abusive relationship, as they almost certainly will lose custody of their children (Human Rights Watch 2015, 68). This is a matter which activists address during the campaign for Lebanon's domestic violence law in 2014, discussed in the next chapter.

Maintenance

Across all religious confessions husbands are required to support wives and children financially. However, in exchange women must cohabit with their husbands and care for their children. In the event of separation or divorce, the husband's duty to provide maintenance expires, following a court ruling terminating the marriage, and if the wife initiates proceedings to terminate the marriage, is recalcitrant, or no longer fulfills her marital obligations. In all confessions, the issuance of a final judgment terminating the marriage suspends a man's obligation to pay spousal maintenance. However, under the Christian and Druze codes a wife can be entitled to damages, but under the Sunni and Shi'ite codes the husband is only limited to paying the deferred *maher*, if the wife did not initiate the divorce (Human Rights Watch 2015).

Marital Property and Inheritance

Lebanese personal status laws do not recognize women's economic and noneconomic contribution to the marriage, including domestic labor. Moreover, there is no community of property in marriage and the family home is considered separately owned and reverts to whose name the property is registered under, which is usually the husbands, although women can own property. Inheritance laws are handled separately for Christians and Muslims in Lebanon. Christian confessions are subject to a non-Islamic law of inheritance, issued on June 23, 1959, under which men and women have equal rights. However, under Islamic inheritance laws, women inherit one-eighth of their husband's property, if there are children and one-quarter if there are not, and female children inherit half the share of their brothers; however, if there are no brothers the remainder is distributed to male agnates. Under the Ja'fari law, male children inherit twice the share of females; however, unlike the Sunni law, if there are no brothers, female children can inherit equally without the property being distributed to male agnates. If there are co-wives they share the one-eighth or one-quarter wives' share, respectively. A husband can inherit one-fourth of the wife's estate if there are children and half if there are no children. While women can own property, nevertheless, they have difficulty proving their contribution toward household effects and property in marriage, in which case it is included as part of the family home, to which they have no entitlement, in the case of a divorce, unless it is in their name (Human Rights Watch 2015; Shehadeh 1998, 510–511). The *maher* is subject to the rules of divorce, as outlined earlier.

SEPARATE AND UNEQUAL WOMEN'S RIGHTS?

Having considered Lebanon's plural system of personal status law, a contradiction arises between designating autonomy to the sects to self-administer family law in religious courts, under Article 9 of the Lebanese constitution, and meeting the obligations Lebanon has under the Convention on the Elimination of All Forms of Discrimination against Women (CEDAW), adopted by the United Nations in 1979, particularly in relation to Articles 9 and 16[4] of this convention, to implement nondiscriminatory nationality and family laws, respectively. Moreover, Lebanon has registered reservations to CEDAW, in relation to these two articles, on the basis that the accepted religious and cultural practices in Lebanon would be adversely affected by compliance with them, despite Lebanon ratifying the convention in 1997 (UNICEF 2006). Tension, therefore, arises between international human rights laws and precepts, based on universalist doctrines and conventions, and the maintenance of a regime of religious difference, embedded within Lebanon's dual legal system. Women's rights are caught in between the two imperatives: first, the right to religious difference, sect (*ta'ifa*) and, second, the obligation to treat women equally, irrespective of their religious affiliation, through their status as citizens (*muwatinin*). Both rights are guaranteed by the constitution. Yet, it has been demonstrated that the Lebanese personal status law system perpetuates the inequality of married women under *femme couverte* (female coverture), because their legal rights are subsumed by those of their husband's (Shehadeh 2010). The system of personal status, thus, is the lynchpin of women's subordination, because women are born free and have equal rights as single women, but lose their legal and civil rights upon marriage, becoming wards of their husband. As Shehadeh argues:

> Having studied the fifteen Lebanese personal-status codes in all their categories of marriage, divorce, guardianship, and custody of children, as well as inheritance, it becomes clear that once a woman gets married, she loses most of her natural and legal rights and the marriage contract emerges as a contract between unequal parties, the husband who is head of the family and the wife who is his ward. (Shehadeh 1998, 511)

However, it is not just the personal status codes, which inscribe married women's inequality and dependence, as civil and secular laws reinforce their inequality in legal capacity, to receive work benefits, employment rights, and abortion rights. Under criminal law, inequality and double standards are evident in honor crime and adultery laws, as well as under nationality law (Shehadeh 1998, 512). Hence, both sides of Lebanon's dual legal system, personal status law on the one hand, and civil and secular laws, on the other, afford women separate and unequal rights in a mutually reinforcing cycle, with the status of married women being the key legal transition, whereby the interests of men over their wives are upheld. For Shehadeh, the key to the problem is that marriage is conceived of as a contract between *unequal* parties, in which women are "bought and sold":

> The marriage contract in Lebanon seems more like that of coverture, where a certain amount of money (*maher*) is paid either to the bride or her family, and a dwelling place is insured together with food and clothing. In return, the wife becomes her husband's sexual property and bears his children and rears them. As such, the man assumes control of the woman's body, which he has literally bought. (Shehadeh 1998, 515)

However, the problem does not reside only within the personal status law system; as such, it is carried forward into the civil law framework, in a second step, which reinforces the unequal exchange of women in marriage (Lerner 1986), inscribed in the marriage contract, to safeguard the dominance of men in the family and society, on the one hand, and the reproduction of sectarian difference, on the other. As was noted in chapter 2, at the heart of the Lebanese constitution a contradiction exists between Article 7, which guarantees the equality of all Lebanese as citizens, and Article 9, which guarantees the absolute freedom of conscience and free exercise of religious rites, with the latter privileged over the former.

The problem for women is that their status is captured within a patriarchal framework, which is reinforced by both religious and secular laws, and the transition in their status occurs at the point of their exchange as brides (from the control of fathers to husbands) and the conversion of their status from single to married women. As single women, they are equal to men in most matters, but after marriage, their bodies are subject to inferior status before civil and secular laws (Shehadeh 1998). Under the criminal penal code there are many laws, which discriminate against women. First, the rape law is a sexual act performed by force on a woman, other than one's wife, which does not recognize marital rape, a point taken up by women's rights activists, as will be discussed in chapter 4; furthermore the perpetrator is absolved of the crime if he marries his victim, under Article 522, which was finally repealed in 2017, following a concerted campaign (Shehadeh 2010).[5] Second, adultery is governed by double standards within the penal code. While a married woman is considered an adulteress, if she is caught and found guilty by the rules of evidence, she receives a sentence between three and twelve months. A man, on the other hand, cannot be found guilty of adultery, if it takes place outside of the marital home; moreover, he would have to flaunt his mistress in public and put his affair in writing to incur a penalty of one to twelve months in prison. If the husband forgives her, a wife's sentence can be commuted. All in all, men have more prerogatives under the law, and the penal code reinforces the power of husbands over their wives. The articles related to honor crimes, or crimes of passion, which enabled a lesser sentence for husbands who committed murder, if they caught their wife committing adultery, were repealed in Lebanon in August 2011, following a concerted campaign by women's rights activist, a point we will return to in the next chapter.

Under the civil code there are further laws which discriminate against women and confirm their inequality as citizens. The first is the labor law, which prescribes several areas of employment in which women are prohibited. Pensions are unequally allocated to men and women, who do not receive family compensation unless they can prove they are a breadwinner, due to having no husband or an incapacitated husband. Upon marriage women's residency and voting rights are transferred to their husband's district and, finally, naturalization and citizenship laws discriminate against Lebanese women. A double standard is practiced, wherein Lebanese men can confer Lebanese citizenship on foreign-born wives, while Lebanese women lose their citizenship upon marriage to a foreign husband, as do their children (Shehadeh 2010). Although naturalized Lebanese women can confer citizenship to their children, upon the death of their husbands, Lebanese-born women cannot. The nationality question is a major campaign of the Lebanese women's movement, which this book will return to in chapter 5.

CONCLUSION

This chapter considered the evolution and practice of the system of plural religious family law in Lebanon and its implications for women's rights. The chapter started by considering the role of women in marriage systems and the anthropological theory that the exchange of women in marriage is the key to their subordination in patriarchal society. The chapter then examined the origins of the system of family law practiced across the Middle Eastern region, the changing dynamics of marriage, and the movement for the reform of personal status law, before turning to the evolution of Lebanon's system of plural religious family law. It was argued that the personal status codes, in practice, can be traced back to the Ottoman Empire and the French Mandate, as well as to the ancient law codes of the region in the pre-Christian and pre-Islamic era, with the first codification of patrilineal descent systems. The chapter then surveyed Lebanon's fifteen separate personal status codes and the differential and unequal rights women experience across all codes. It is evident that both Christian and Muslim personal status codes produce and reproduce inequality between the sexes and do not consider the best interest of the child, following the dissolution of marriage. Given the role of the marriage contract in establishing the coverture of married women in Lebanon, it is to the marriage contract itself that women's rights activists must turn in their efforts to equalize women's legal rights within the family and citizenship rights within the nation. Through the reform of personal status laws, and the introduction of an optional unified civil status code, the marriage contract can be rewritten from a contract between unequal parties, based on religious difference, to an equal contract between citizens. While some may argue that repealing the discriminatory laws is insufficient to change women's status in Lebanon (Shehadeh 1998), is it a necessary step to make other reforms possible? To answer this question, the next part of the book examines four contemporary women's rights campaigns in Lebanon, from domestic violence, nationality, and political rights to the reform of family law and civil marriage.

NOTES

1. 1950s, when women were granted to travel without the approval of a male guardian (Stephan 2012a).

2. See the following article: https://www.straitstimes.com/world/middle-east/sau dis-blast-guardianship-laws-after-womans-escape.

3. The notice of divorce should be lodged with the *Shari'a* court within fifteen days, as well as the Department of Personal Status, but it is not invalidated if it is not

but the husband could be subject to criminal penalty (Dr. An-An-aim. Islamic Family Law, Lebanon scholar blog).

4. CEDAW list of articles, UN Women. Article 9: Nationality, "Women have equal rights with men to acquire, change or retain their nationality and that of their children." Article 16, "Women have equal rights with men within marriage including family planning, property ownership and occupation." See full convention here: http://www.un.org/womenwatch/daw/cedaw/text/econvention.htm#article4.

5. See https://www.bbc.com/news/world-middle-east-40947448.

Part II

ACTIVISM

Having examined the formation of the women's rights puzzle in Lebanon in the first part of the book, part II of the book examines the Lebanese women's movement and a new phase of activism, which accelerated after 2011. Chapter 4 starts by examining the history of Lebanese women's movement, the rise of new modes of online/offline activism in the context of the Arab Spring, and the role of new media technologies in the mobilization for social change. The case of Lebanon's domestic violence law in 2014 is surveyed. Chapter 5 expands the analysis to consider the intersectional relationship between women's rights activism and civil rights campaigns, by examining three key campaigns: the women's nationality campaign, the women's quota in parliament, and the #YouStink campaign. Lastly, chapter 6 explores Lebanon's contentious civil marriage debate, following the first civil marriage on Lebanese soil in 2013 and asks, can civil marriage resolve Lebanon's confessional contradictions and improve women's rights?

Chapter 4

A New Phase of Women's Rights Activism

Online and Offline

INTRODUCTION

This chapter examines online/offline women's rights activism in Lebanon, which has bypassed old media channels to promote their message and bring about legislative change. The upsurge in citizen's rights campaigns across the Middle East, since the start of the Arab Spring in 2011, highlighted the role of women in the new social movements, and revived the feminist scholarly debate on the relationship between citizen's rights and women's rights in processes of social transformation, as noted in chapter 1. While the critical role of new media technologies in facilitating the new social movements has been widely debated, fewer studies have collected empirical data on women's online campaigns, in the Arab uprisings, or asked activists themselves their views on the efficacy of online versus offline modes of social mobilization. This chapter contributes to the conversation by analyzing online/offline women's rights activism in Lebanon. The chapter considers whether new media technologies have enabled the Lebanese women's movement to bring about legislative change. The chapter starts with an examination of the history of the Lebanese women's movement, then considers the latest phase of women's rights activism. A case study online/offline campaign to pass a domestic violence law in 2014[1] is presented. The findings suggest that no one mode of activism was superior to the other, but rather, the iterative dynamism between the two modes of activism led to significant reforms in women's rights, despite Lebanon's state of political paralysis. However, given the intersectional nature of the women's rights puzzle in Lebanon, further social change is necessary to improve women's equality overall.

NEW MEDIA AND SOCIAL CHANGE
IN THE ARAB SPRING

New media technologies have been central to the new social movements of the Arab Spring and, according to Hirst and Harrison (2007, 234), can be defined as a "catchall phrase used to distinguish digital media forms from old media, such as newspapers magazines, radio, and television." Social media, however, refers more specifically to digital media, either web or mobile based, which integrate telecommunications and social interaction and are based on web. 2.0 technologies, which allow for the creation and exchange of user-generated content and include Skype, Facebook, Twitter, MSN, You-Tube, LinkedIn, and WhatsApp, to name a few (Fisher 2009).

Digital convergence, according to Flew (2008, 2), "arises in the first instance out of the growing linkages between media, information technology and telecommunications." The concept of convergence, according to Jenkins (2008, 2–3), refers to the flow of content across multiple media platforms but also should be understood as a cultural shift, whereby consumers are encouraged to seek out new information from disparate media sources, as active participants in the production and circulation of information. The three 'C's of convergent new media are computer networks, computer information technology, and content media (Flew 2008, 10). The development of convergence, digitization, and the networked society rapidly accelerated after the consolidation of the Internet during the mid-1990s, first in the postindustrial countries of the North and now in the global South. Indeed, Flew (2008, 15) argues that the Internet has been the fastest-growing medium ever. The period between the development of the Internet and its adoption by 50 million users in the United States, for example, was five years, as opposed to thirteen for television and thirty-eight for radio. According to Castells, this transformation has led to a new mode of development, following his network society thesis, based on the accumulation and exchange of information (in Hirst and Harrison 2007, 48).

The attempt, however, to regulate the Internet and social media points to less glossy alternate digital futures, according to Hirst and Harrison (2007, 294), based not on the democratizing potential of digital revolution, but on what they refer to, following Foucault (in Hirst and Harrison 2007, 300), as the rise of the "surveillance society," based on "greater levels of physical and electronic surveillance of citizens." Its distinguishing feature, they argue, is the role of new media technologies in normalizing overt and extensive surveillance, which is both internalized as self-censorship and democratized, because we all can Google and, thus, spy on each other (Hirst and Harrison 2007, 302).

Until the Arab Spring, however, the literature on new media (Alonso and Oiarzabal 2010; Awan et al. 2011; Buckingham and Willett 2006) and digital convergence (Jenkins 2008) focused largely on the Western hemisphere and the postindustrial knowledge economies of the global North (Flew 2008, 2; Covell 2000; Hirst and Harrison 2007; Donk 2004; Chester 2007; Naib 2011). Less attention has been paid to the impact of digital convergence on the countries of the global South (Alonso and Oiarzabal 2010). However, the uprisings and revolutions, across the Middle East, since 2011, have focused scholarly attention on the primacy, or not, of social media in bringing about social transformation. While there are optimistic accounts of the link between digital revolution and the process of democratization (Noueihed and Warren 2012, 44–45), authoritarian and democratic regimes alike are sensitive to the power of social media and have attempted to regulate it, control it, or even shut down the Internet, as was the case in Egypt on the January 28, 2011, Syria on February 5, 2011, and even during the British riots in August 2011 (Goodman 2011) or Iran in 2019.

Following Marx, some scholars argue that revolutions represent a complete reordering of the political, social, and economic order, while Arendt distinguishes between the political and economic dimensions of revolutions (Dabashi 2012, 59–61). However, in the Arab Spring, one of the main debates among scholars of New Media is the relationship between technology and social change and the primacy of human action over technology, or vice versa, in instigating the process of social change (Giddens 1991; Flew 2008; Hirst and Harrison 2007). The privileging of technology over human agency in social change theory is argued to be a form of technological determinism (McGuigan 2007). Alternately, Flew (2008) argues, that digital convergence should be seen as part of an epochal shift in global capitalism, along with globalization, toward interactivity, connectivity, and virtuality, particularly in the information and service-based economy (Flew 2008, 208).

Likewise, in the Arab Spring, scholars debated whether technology or human agency was primarily responsible for bringing about the social transformations (Flew 2008; Harrison and Hirst 2007). Barkawi (2011) posited that human agency causes revolutions, not telecommunication technologies per se. Likewise, Perry theorized that ideas spark revolution, but social media technologies help sustain them and accelerate the circulation of revolutionary ideas by allowing protesters to circumvent censorship in order to organize (Perry 2011). Contrary to the technological determinism thesis, the information infrastructure, especially mobile phone use, was found to be vital to the success of the revolutionary social movements (Howard and Hussain 2013, 48–49):

> It is wrong headed to construct a technologically deterministic theory of contemporary democratization, but it is good social science to critically assess the role of tools that have enabled both social movement leaders and empowered recalcitrant dictators. (Howard and Hussain 2013, 50)

Building on this point, Turner (2013, 379–380) argues that new media technology has been an effective tool of mobilization, particularly for new social movements, with a radical orientation, which aim to alter the scope of authority or even replace it.

After early optimism, the Arab Spring is considered by some scholars to be a work in progress (Ahmed and Macharia 2013), to have stalled, or turned into an Arab Winter,[2] as noted in chapter 1. Despite the predictions of revolutions stalled, postponed, or overturned, in Lebanon several significant women's rights advancements, legislative breakthroughs, and transformations have occurred, as a result of women's online/offline activism since 2013, despite extended periods of political deadlock in the political process.

THE DEVELOPMENT OF THE LEBANESE WOMEN'S MOVEMENT

I take a broad, pluralistic view of what constitutes a women's movement, following Arenfeldt and Al-Hassan (2012, 8–13), including formal and informal organizations, with and without an explicit feminist agenda and both collective and individual modes of activism, which together have improved gender equity. While the first women's rights organizations (WROs) emerged in what is now Lebanon in the early 1900s, during the first phase of the Lebanese women's movements, as noted in chapter 1, women's organizations also played a significant role in the movement for decolonization in Lebanon (Stephan 2012, 114). However, a second phase of women's rights activism emerged following independence in 1943. The Lebanese women's movement at this time had its roots in the women's charitable associations of the post–World War II era, which were firmly part of the *haute bourgeoisie* (Stephan 2010, 535) and were embedded in the sectarian family structure of Lebanese society, as represented by the of Lebanese Council of Women (Stephan 2010, 535). This phase of feminist activists, such as Laure Moghaizel, focused on women's suffrage rights,[3] female mobility to travel without the permission of their husbands,[4] female reproductive rights, and access to contraception.[5] Stephan (2010, 535) characterizes their approach to feminism as "family feminism," which worked within the kinship structure of Lebanese society and often in conjunction with their husbands. The third phase of the Lebanese women's movement emerged from the ashes of the civil war in 1990, as this women's rights activist explains:

> The women's movement was shattered because the women were stuck taking care of the wounded, fighting, and trying to stop the war. Then in the early 90s, it started to come back, and in 1995 there was the big Beijing Conference, after which a lot of organizations started to work actively. The first topic they

worked on, after 1995, was violence against women. And I think that's where all feminist movements start. (Interview with Nasawiya activist, Beirut May 2012)

The women's movement flowered after the United Nations International Women's Conference in Beijing in 1995 (UN Women), which led to the ratification of CEDAW (UN Women 2009) by Lebanon in 1996 (Stephan 2012a). In this period, many WROs were formed, such as KAFA (enough violence against women), Collective for Research and Training on Development-Action (CRTD.A), Bahithat, Najdeh, ABAAD Resource Centre for Gender Equality, the Non-Governmental National Committee for the Follow-Up of Women's Issues (post-Beijing), and Justice Without Frontiers. Some of these WROs have links to international agencies, such as Oxfam, the European Union, and the United Nations. Universal human rights and the UN's Sustainable Development Goals were translated into the local context through WROs on the ground (Sabat 2012). One interviewee and academic noted the following point, regarding the translation of the international rights agenda into the Lebanese context, during this time:

> I think, in Lebanon and in any other country where you would study women's rights movements, you will see a sort of negotiation between what is written in documents on the international level and how women translate them onto the ground. The first negotiation that has to take place is between a women's activist and herself and her community and how it is written in the international level. So, I think, there is a uniqueness to the Lebanese women's activism simply by the nature of being part of Lebanon and having a value system that they must actually put in line. (Interview, Beirut 2012)

Still others consider that the Lebanese women's movement reflects a generational timeline:

> It is not a question of generations; it is more of a timeline and in terms of the political context at the time: post-independence in the 50s, in the 70s in the civil war, and Beijing in the 90s and with the end of the Civil War, and the present day. It invariably becomes generations, but it is a timeline. (Interview, Beirut July 2012)

One of the main points that activists make about the range of WROs in Lebanon is that they tend to be directed by the sources of their funding and this determines the topography of the movement, whether they were independent or not, as this activist from the CRTD.A comments:

> It is like the rise of women's movements throughout region, in between the off shoots of the political parties, the leftist parties notably, were definitely the pioneers, and not that they made the breakthrough in terms of equality, but in terms of having off-shoots in women's organizations, and those who are close to the

confessional system, and donor-dependent and then more or less independent groups like KAFA, CRTD.A. In a way, it is a topography. (Interview, Beirut July 2012)

Thus, for some there is no Lebanese women's movement in terms of unified priorities and objectives, but rather activists and sectors, working on particular issues. Hence, following social movement theory, as outlined in chapter 1, there is no women's movement in Lebanon but rather an informal network of women's organizations and activists who access limited funds from donors and are divided into specific campaigns, as ABAAD explains:

> We should engage the young, because it is a new phase and a new way to address women's issues. . . . There is no women movement *per se* in Lebanon, you can say women's activism. But not a kind of a movement in the sense that we have the same agenda and the same priorities, same objectives . . . every group is working on and focusing on one sector more or less . . . and funding is not sufficient among everyone. There is a difference between the new groups that are using social media and new techniques and using new campaigning tools then those who are older. (Interview, Beirut July 2012)

Building on the work of the third phase of the Lebanese women's movement, a fourth phase of the women's movement started in Lebanon in 2005 (Stephan 2012b, 2014), after the Spring Revolution, following the assassination of Rafiq Hariri and the movement for the withdrawal of Syrian troops from Lebanon. In this phase of women's rights activism, I identify an explicitly feminist discourse and an intersectional approach to women's inequality, which links women's rights and civil rights. The campaigns have deployed new online/offline activism strategies, utilizing social media technologies, while the underlying issues they campaign to change have been carried forward from the third phase of women's rights activism in Lebanon.

The new intersectional phase of activism consolidated after 2010–2011, led by the organization *Nasawiya*, an online feminist collective, which defined itself as a new and more radical phase of Lebanese feminism. They have three key pillars of action: to create feminist initiatives, to connect marginalized groups with activists, and to support social change with resources for action. They reflect a new phase of Lebanese feminism:

> This period 2010–2011 is a new phase of Lebanese feminism. I think it's been changing so much, and it is becoming a lot more focused on change, real change. Before 2010 the women's movement never talked about sectarianism,

although it's such a big challenge to what we are doing. (*Nasawiya* activist. Interview, Beirut May 2012)

Stephan (2014) characterizes the new phase of feminist activism as "gendered democracy," while Naber and Zaatarie (2014) traced the nascent emergence of *Nasawiya* and new phase activists in their research on the impact of the 2006 Israeli invasion of Lebanon on feminist and LGBTQ activism. They argue that the state of emergency imposed by the war foreclosed activism, as saving lives, not challenging sexualities became the priority, and patriarchal social structures were accentuated in the context of war and imperialism (Naber and Zaatarie 2014, 96). But this was only a pause, as such, and the state of emergency which has become the new normal (Hermez 2011) didn't foreclose the development of a new and more radical phase of Lebanese feminism:

> But now, it is becoming a lot clearer that we are against the sectarian system, and the warlords . . . so we have to do something more radical and I think with *Nasawiya* coming along in 2010, it was a new phase. (*Nasawiya* activist. Interview, Beirut May 2012)

This contrasts with the malaise of the secular left in general in Lebanon, according to Hermez (2011), which struggled to develop a new politics in the aftermath of the decline of the Soviet Union, the rise of the Islamic resistance, and the emergence of the NGO agenda. However, for the new phase of feminist activists in Lebanon, new media provided the platform for the development of a more radical feminist critique of Lebanese state and society, which gained momentum ahead of the official start of the Arab Spring. Importantly, new phase activists recognize the intersectional relationship between women's rights and secular citizenship in Lebanon, as their core project. This interviewee explains the link between the women's movement and civil rights:

> Women's issues are very much damaged by the sectarian system, women get the worst treatment because of the sectarian system. And they see that. It is very obvious for us. You've got 15 different rules and sets of regulations, and so if you can't unite the sects, how are you going to unite the women's movement? It is disastrous. And, it hits where the woman hurts the most; with divorce, custody, and personal status issues. This is where the pain is, inside the families and inside the families are controlled by the religious courts, and it must stop, it has to be civil courts, it has to be objective, it can't be: "God taught you to be good to your husband." We have to get out of that mentality. (*Nasawiya* activist. Interview, Beirut May 2012)

A distinctively intersectional Lebanese feminism is articulated, therefore, which defines itself as being both feminist and secular, a point of view expressed clearly in this comment on the nature of the feminist struggle in Lebanon:

> According to me, the Lebanese feminist movement has to defend women rights, but in the same time, it's defending secularism and equality in Lebanese society, not only for women, but for every Lebanese citizen and non-Lebanese citizen, such as migrant workers. (Open text comment: Online social media survey 2012)

The online survey of social media and the Lebanese women's movement, outlined in the introduction, asked respondents whether Lebanese feminism could be classified as liberal, socialist, radical, or faith based and the majority of respondents felt that none of these classical divisions from Western feminism/s applied to Lebanese feminism. While 73 percent of respondents identified as being feminist, an intersectional approach is favored, which recognizes the intertwined nature of the woman's rights puzzle in Lebanon. Consequently, when asked in the online survey on social media and the Lebanese women's rights movement (2012), to rank-order the most important women's rights issues in Lebanon, women's citizenship and nationality rights were ranked highest, followed by a domestic violence law, the reform of personal status codes, civil marriage, the women's quota in cabinet, and the reform of inheritance laws (see figure 4.1).

The key issues debated by the fourth phase of the Lebanese women's movement have been carried forward from the third phase; however, the tools to tackle the problems have changed. While women's equal citizenship rights are ranked highest, consistent with the intersectional focus, the low representation of women in parliament is a key problem, with Lebanon ranked 183rd in the world (IPU 2019), a topic we return to in the next chapter. Women's rights activists have been debating a 30 percent women's quota to redress the problem and force social change using the fast-track model, since the Beijing 1995 platform for action (Dahelrup 2009, 30). The domestic violence law was legislated in 2014 and ranked second, which will be analyzed in this chapter. The reform of personal status codes ranked third, including civil marriage, and will be examined in chapter 6, with mixed results. Moreover, the *Nasawiya* feminist collective explains why Lebanese women need citizenship and nationality rights as a matter of top priority because:

> We're not really Lebanese citizens; we're just the daughters of Lebanese men. Because if we really did possess a Lebanese citizenship, we'd be able to pass our nationality to our husbands and children; but we can't?[6]

Rank the most important women's rights issues in Lebanon

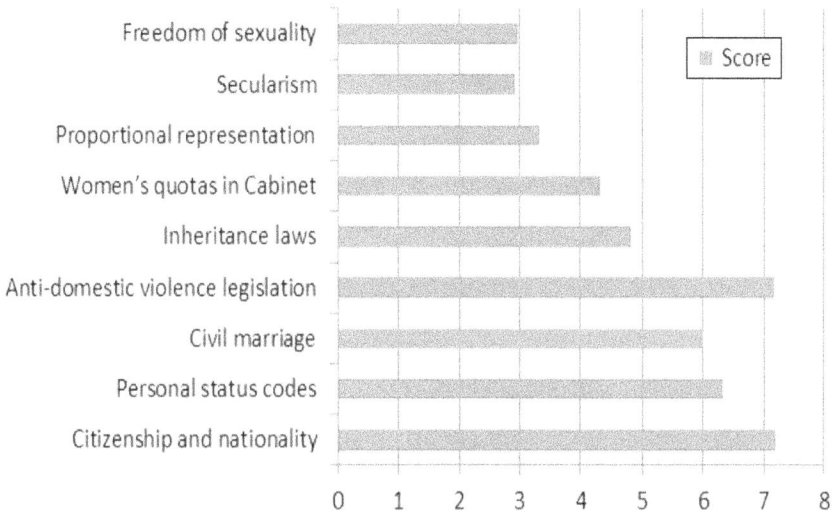

Figure 4.1   **Ranking of Women's Rights Issues in Lebanon.** *Source*: Online social media and women's activism survey 2012.

This explanation sums up the core of the women's rights puzzle in Lebanon. Without full citizenship rights, Lebanese women do not belong to the nation, and as long as the nation denies women their full citizenship rights, it will remain a nation divided by sect. Given the interrelationship between the confessional system and the women's rights deficit in Lebanon, the campaigns of the fourth phase of Lebanese women's movement address both elements of the women's rights puzzle in Lebanon. While the questions new phase activists address are not new, their strategies to bring about social change are; we will now examine the strategies and tools deployed in the online campaign.

STRATEGIES FOR ONLINE ACTIVISM

The most important new campaign strategy utilized by the new phase of feminist activists in Lebanon is the extensive utilization of new media technologies, both mobile and web-based. The respondents to the online survey of social media and Lebanese women's movement[7] were from a variety of backgrounds. They were overwhelmingly women, 98 percent, and 91 percent were born in Lebanon. They were from a variety of religious backgrounds, with 25 percent identifying as being Muslim, 32 percent Christian, and 40 percent were not-religious. The remainder identified as following another religion. Their ages ranged from those born in the early 1950s, to those born in the mid-1990s. They spoke a number of languages, with 99 percent speaking Arabic and English, respectively, followed by 76 percent speaking French and 12 percent speaking Spanish. Typical of Lebanon's high rates of emigration, while 78 percent of the respondents now live in Lebanon permanently, 57 percent have lived outside of the country, with France being the most common country of residence, followed by America, Canada, West Africa, the Arab Gulf States, Australia, and the United Kingdom; a smaller number have lived in South America. They were also highly educated, with 47 percent having a Bachelor's degree and 50 percent having a postgraduate degree. The majority of respondents identified as being feminists, 72 percent, while 79 percent identified as being activists.

The online survey found that the home computer was the most common platform to access the Internet, based on the largest number of responses, followed by smart phones and then computers in workplaces. This reflects the rise of the smart phone and mobile cellular Internet in the last decade, while home was still the most frequent location for online activity (see figure 4.2). When asked which smart phone they used, 57 percent of respondents to the online survey used iPhones, followed by Windows phones, with 26 percent of users, while Blackberries came last, with only 17 percent of users. The switch to smart phones can be attributed to the high cost of home-based Internet plans in Lebanon and the slow speed. Indeed, 82 percent of respondents to the online survey agreed that Lebanon has a digital divide problem in terms of access to the Internet. When

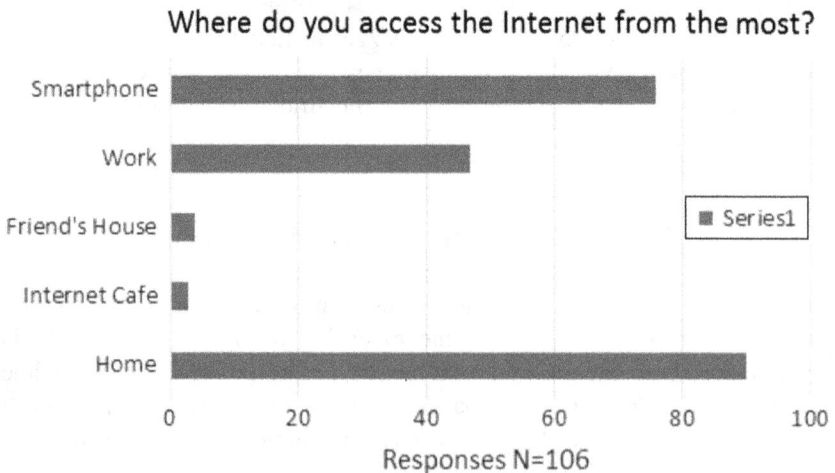

Figure 4.2 Access to the Internet. *Source*: Online Survey of Social Media 2012.

asked what the elements of that divide were, the speed of the Internet in Lebanon received the highest number of responses (sixty-two), followed by knowledge of computers (fifty-seven), age (forty-three), location in rural areas, education, the language spoken online, and income (see figure 4.3). According to the online survey, English is by far the most dominant online language among respondents, with 79 percent of respondents reporting that they use English online, and only 15 percent reporting they use Arabic, while 7 percent reported they use French. This shows that, while activists themselves are highly engaged with online activism, access to the Internet is not evenly distributed in Lebanon between rural and urban areas, or between age or language groups. The dominance of English language online is also a barrier to wider engagement with the online world. By contrast, as was evident from the survey results, technology is also an equalizer, as it enables activists to reach audiences they previously couldn't and promote their campaigns in new modes and on new platforms, which are not dominated by the mainstream media or political establishment.

When asked about their online activity, the top four activities were utilizing social media, reading online news, email, and online activism (see figure 4.4). The online survey also found that Facebook was the most common social media application among 97 percent of survey respondents.

A picture emerges, from the online survey of social media and the Lebanese women's movement, of a young, mobile, interconnected, polyglot group of activists, who are highly educated, and utilize smart phone and computer-based Internet to access social media apps to communicate and network with each other, to access news, and engage in online activism.

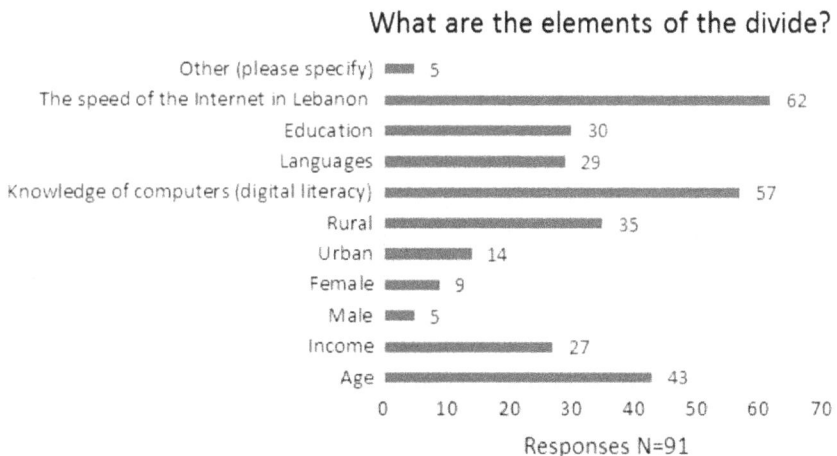

Figure 4.3 Elements of the Digital Divide in Lebanon. *Source*: Online Social Media Survey 2012.

What do you do online?

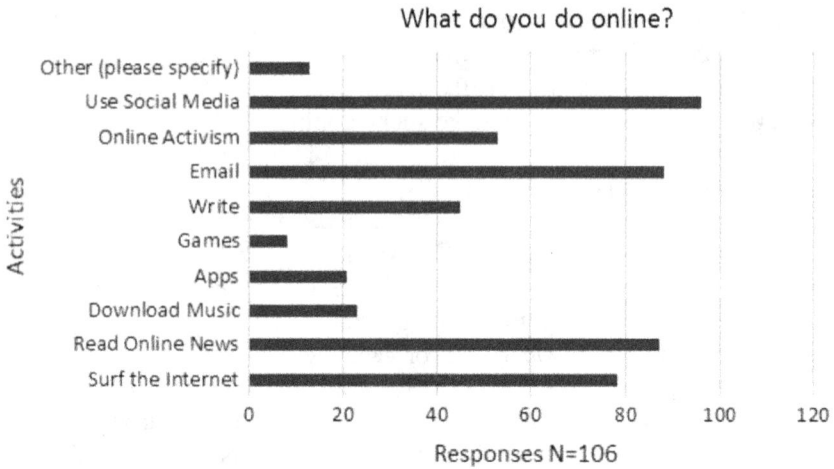

Responses N=106

Figure 4.4 Online Activity. *Source*: Social Media Online Survey.

Which online strategies are most effective?

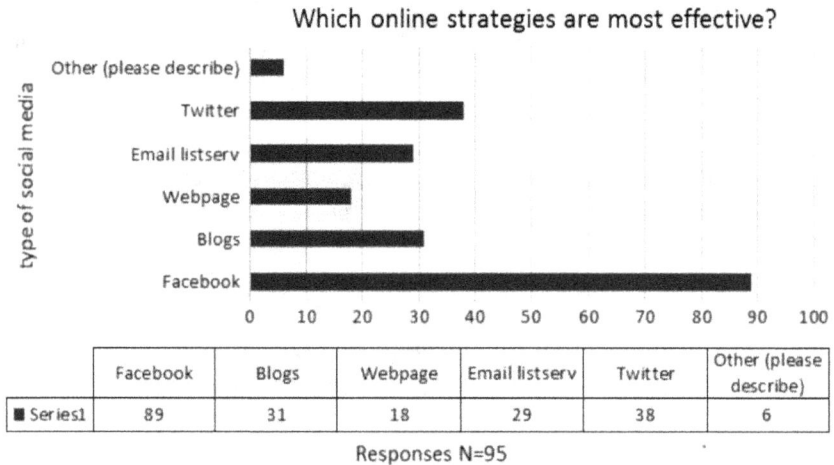

	Facebook	Blogs	Webpage	Email listserv	Twitter	Other (please describe)
■ Series1	89	31	18	29	38	6

Responses N=95

Figure 4.5 Social Media Effectiveness for Online Campaigns. *Source*: Social media survey 2013.

In total, 84 percent of respondents reported they use online strategies to advocate for women's rights. When asked which social media apps were the most effective for online activism, Facebook had the highest number of responses, followed by Twitter, Blogs, Email Listserv, and, finally, Webpages (see figure 4.5).

Why does social media have such appeal to activists? In order to answer the question, thirty face-to-face interviews with activists were carried out,

How effective are online campaigns?

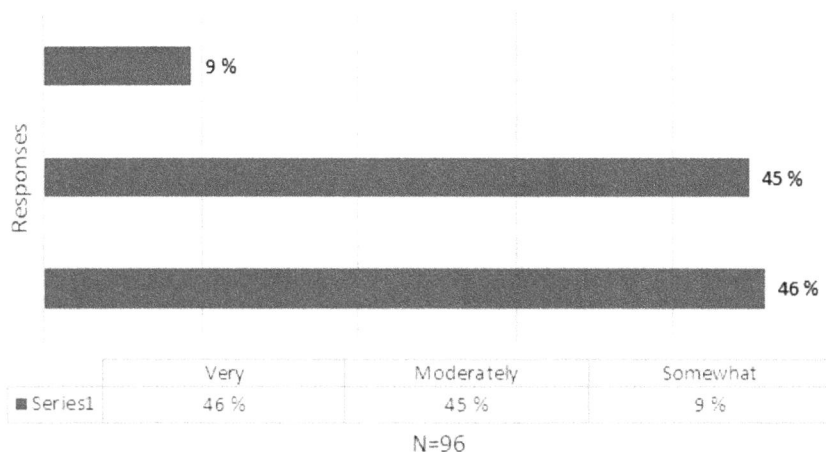

Figure 4.6 **Effectiveness of Online Campaigns.** *Source*: Online Survey of Social Media 2012.

to understand the role of online activism in the contemporary Lebanese women's movement. A key finding is that the unregulated space, which new media offers, relative to old media, is the key to its appeal, as well as its broad potential audience in Lebanon. It is free, unregulated, open access, and, thus, has a wide distribution, which rivals traditional media:

> We cannot pay for traditional media, or billboards, or TV ads, or radio ads, or magazine ads, etc. But social media is free. And the great thing is that all these traditional media are following us to social media. Nasawiya specifically, we started using social media because we didn't have another choice. (*Nasawiya* activist. Interview, Beirut May 2012)

The interviewee goes on to argue that the most important aspect of the online campaign is its democratizing potential to provide open access to information. That is, if it is "online" it is published, read, distributed, and the ideas are shared, and this is a threat to the mainstream media:

> It doesn't matter where I put my article, if I put it on my Blog, it doesn't mean it gets fewer visitors than if I put it on Akhbar English. It doesn't matter anymore where it is or who the headline is, you can have more credibility as an activist than CNN and that's what the news agencies are struggling with. (*Nasawiya* activist. Interview, Beirut May 2012)

As for the technology and social change debate, is human agency or technology the driving force behind social change, according to online activists themselves? The interviewee puts forward her view on this debate and argues that new media technologies are just a new tool to build mobilization for social change:

> I think it would be naive to think that social media brings about social change. We have established that, in the same way a telephone cannot bring about social change or a microwave. These are tools. And they can support you immensely, but in different ways. It cannot be the one thing you will be doing the whole day on the laptop. You have to have work on the ground, so social change would manifest. (*Nasawiya* activist. Beirut May 2012)

The critical link, as this interviewee explained, is that the online and offline campaign must be synchronized and materialized in social action on the ground, in the form of street demonstrations and, ultimately, legislative change. The findings of the online survey support this view with 97 percent of respondents supporting the proposition that online campaigns need to be followed up with action on the ground and 46 percent thought that online campaigns were very successful, while another 45 percent thought they were moderately successful and 9 percent somewhat successful (see figure 4.6). In all, activists who responded to the online survey had a positive view of the effectiveness of online activism strategies to bring about social change, yet the online and offline modes of activism need to be integrated if social change is to be materialized and legislated.

I argue that the ability to use the online sphere to promote real change in the offline sphere, and the iterative movement between the two, has been crucial to the success of the new phase of feminist activism in Lebanon. Indeed, Turner (2013, 380–381) has also noted the recursive relationship between online and offline social movements, which enhance their tools for mobilization by using web 2.0 technologies to synchronize the two modes of activism. In the case of Lebanon, however, I argue the online mode of activism has been a particularly significant tool to overcome the perennial security problems, which foreclosed the possibilities for activism in the past (Hermez 2011). However, I suggest that the iterative movement between online and offline activism enables a steady movement forward, despite recurring political deadlocks between 2013 and 2018.

However, translating online activity into on-the-ground mobilization is not always a linear transition. Indeed, one activist noted that while it might appear that people are enthusiastic online about the campaign, it does not always translate into action, as was her experience with the civil marriage campaign: "I was part of the optional civil marriage campaign, it is always great online but when it comes to mobilizing people for action in reality you find them less available" (response to Online Survey on Social Media, 2012). Online comments noted that some participants saw themselves as feminists but not activists, suggesting they are more inclined to be "armchair" campaigners. It is easier to like a page than it is to get out on the streets.

Others considered Blogs to be the most effective tool, in addition to a Facebook page, as it maintains an intensive impact, while Twitter is also helpful to spread the news and keep people updated with the campaign's progress. An online campaign focused on CEDAW was very effective on Facebook, an activist shared, because of the power of visual images and photos for building sympathy and interest. Another activist, involved with One Billion and Rising in Lebanon, utilized a Facebook campaign to organize a smart mob as part of an international campaign. The action and on-the-ground event mobilized against domestic violence. While there are those who question the influence of the online campaign on offline action, there are others who conclude that overall:

> The online campaign succeeded. I have 1400 friends of FB and from the likes, comments and the shares of some related pictures and statuses, I can tell that people are influenced and affected by what I post and not only my friends, but also their friends as well. (online comments to Social Media Survey 2012)

While the success, in this case, is measured by online activity, we turn now to the case of Lebanon's domestic violence law, which was passed in 2014, following an extensive online/offline campaign, which resulted in a legislative change on the ground.

THE CASE OF PASSING DOMESTIC VIOLENCE LAW 293

The rate of domestic violence in Lebanon is high, although it is likely to be underreported. In 2014 KAFA, a nongovernmental organization (NGO), which advocates for women against domestic violence and abuse, received 2,600 reports of domestic abuse and reported that from 2010 to 2013, twenty-five women were killed by a family member in Lebanon (Human Rights Watch 2014). In 2010, it was reported that 55 percent of women in Lebanon were exposed to physical or verbal abuse (Human Rights Watch 2014), while a 2015 report by the United National Population Fund (UNFPA) reports that 50 percent of the population personally know someone subject to domestic violence and 65 percent of reported incidents were committed by family members (UNFPA 2015).

The passing of Lebanon's Law 293 on the Protection of Women and Family Members from Domestic Violence, on April 1, 2014, followed years of online/offline advocacy by *KAFA*.[8] It was first introduced as a draft law in 2010, with support from a wide range of other civil society and WROs in Lebanon, including *Nasawiya* and *ABAAD*. One activist describes the operation of the online campaign throughout 2012 to bring pressure on the government to pass the law:

> We were monitoring regular news about gender-based violence and women rights violations, and posting them along with pictures and videos, invitations to events, and articles on Facebook. We also put ads on Facebook to promote the campaign and worked on encouraging our page fans, including NGO members, activists, women and friends, to spread the information about different forms of gender- based violence, and the Law to Protect Women from Family Violence. We worked through our two months project to spread the information we were posting as much as possible. We worked in every event on informing activists and NGOs working on this issue about our advocacy campaign, building a sustainable relationship with them and gaining their support. Knowing that the number of people who saw our posts during this period was more than 15000 individuals and the number of people who shared and liked these posts was more than 3000. Note that, we not only participated in the events organized by activists and NGOs and mobilized people through our Facebook page, but also, we broadcasted individual, personalized messages through our mailing list, which includes 12000 emails. Without forgetting also, the pressure we succeeded to create, through monitoring women rights violations and spreading them among the general public, which gave the issue of gender based violence a big exposure through mass and social media. (Open text response: Online Survey 2012)

Following another year of inertia in Lebanese politics in 2013, which only had a caretaker government at the time, and the prominent murder of three Lebanese women in domestic violence cases, a record number of protesters attended the International Women's Day demonstration on March 8, 2014, in downtown Beirut[9] and maximum pressure was placed on lawmakers at the first sitting of the newly formed cabinet to pass the law. Despite attempts to water it down, particularly the marital rape provision, the law was passed as the first act of the new Lebanese government on April 1, 2014.[10] Thus, the new phase of activists successfully combined their online and offline campaigns to bring about legislative change.

Prior to Law 293, there was no law against domestic violence on the books, although Article 562 of the Penal Code, which reduced the penalty for honor crimes, was repealed in 2011, as noted in chapter 3 (UNDP 2018b). While the passing of the law was a huge step forward, ABAAD and *Nasawiya* activists felt that the law did not go far enough and fell short in key areas. The law did, however, establish new protections and court reforms, which included the ability for women to get a restraining order against an abuser, the establishment of temporary shelters for victims, the assignment of public prosecutor for each governorate to receive complaints and investigate domestic violence, and the establishment of specialized domestic violence units within Lebanon's domestic police, or Internal Security Forces. The law defines domestic violence as "An act, act of omission, or threat of an act committed by a family member against one or more family members . . . related to one of the crimes stipulated in this law, and that results in killing, harm, or physical, psychological, sexual, or economic harm" (Human Rights Watch 2014).

The immediate criticisms were that the law defined domestic violence too narrowly, thus, it did not include all forms of abuse, including assault, which is left to the Penal Code. The most pressing criticism, however, was that the law did not include a marital rape provision, as noted earlier, which was removed from the draft law, due to objections from religious authorities, while a reference to the "marital right of intercourse" was included. As Lebanon is a signatory to the Convention on the Elimination of all forms of Discrimination Against Women (CEDAW), which called on Lebanon to criminalize marital rape, this was considered a major watering down of the law. Lastly, Article 22 of the new law states that all provisions considered contrary to Lebanon's personal status law will be annulled, except in the case it undermines women's security. Other key findings relating to the progress of the law are that the law does not protect refugee women in Lebanon, whose population is significant, and that the courts of urgent matters, which deal with domestic violence orders, have limited capacity and, finally, a general lack of awareness of Law 293 prevails in Lebanon today (Moussawi and Yassin 2017). As of 2017, 175 official protection orders were released and another fourteen Lebanese women were killed in domestic crimes since the law was passed. Consequently, KAFA drafted an amendment to the law, which has not been passed (Human Rights Watch 2014).

What is noted is that domestic violence intersects with a range of other gender justice issues for Lebanese women, which together prevent women from leaving abusive relationships. First, social and cultural norms across Lebanon's religious communities favor the maintenance of the family unit. Second, many economic barriers prevent women from leaving a violent relationship, as there is no alternative than the marital home (Moussawi and Yassin 2017). While Lebanon has a high female literacy rate, 91.8 percent, the labor force participation rate is low at 23 percent, as noted in the preface (World Bank 2019), so women find themselves financially dependent on their spouse. Finally, leaving abusive relationships is made worse by women's tenuous status within the system of plural personal status law, which restricts women's maternal custody rights and access to divorce or alimony, as outlined in chapter 3, making leaving abusive relationships a high-risk option, as they will likely lose custody of their children. As one respondent to the online survey on civil marriage attitudes noted,

> A lot of religious marriages enable the males to dominate in the relationship and encourage rights for men, while subduing the role of women in the relationship. This makes marriage more difficult and can backfire on women . . . if they seek a divorce, their kids are taken from them and they have no ownership [of property]. (Open text comment: Online civil marriage survey 2012)

As shown in chapter 3, broader issues of gender-based violence include the marriage of girls under the age of eighteen, which is permitted under Lebanon's personal status laws (UNDP 2018b), which varies across the codes. Violence, in the view of activists, is not just a problem within the family but is a structural problem within the state, due to the structure of the laws and codes, which are highly discriminating against women and lock them into abusive relationships, with little alternative, as this respondent to the online survey on civil marriage reform notes:

> Personal status laws and codes that are issued by sectarian communities, leaders and religious authorities are highly discriminative towards women. They are imposed upon women, forcing them to follow codes whether they like it or not, which is a form of symbolic violence by our state. (Open text comment: Online Survey of Civil Marriage Attitudes, 2013)

LESSONS LEARNED

A year after the legislation was passed, activists were still debating the viability of the legislation, considering the nonrecognition of marital rape. In the end, activists concluded that the new law, while a first step, still has a way to go before it is fully applied (Moussawi and Yasin 2017). Human Rights Watch (2014) also took the view that the new law was good, but incomplete, in relation to the strength of restraining orders. Nonetheless, with the passing of Law 293, for the first time, several violent male spouses were arrested and tried for killing their wives, in several widely publicized legal cases in the Lebanese media, demonstrating that women's rights are moving in the right direction, because of the legislative change. While the significant achievement was passing Law 293, especially during a political impasse, the protections offered by the law can be further consolidated with the adoption of other reforms to family law. The online/offline strategy assisted in gaining social media attention on the domestic violence question and resulted in a large street mobilization on International Women's Day in 2014,[11] which pushed the parliament to pass the legislation the next month. Due to the intersectional nature of the women's rights puzzle in Lebanon, one campaign leads to another. Without significant reform of the personal status codes, which would make leaving a violent relationship easier, many activists believe that tackling domestic violence will remain an incomplete task.

CONCLUSION

In this chapter I explored the rise of women's online activism in Lebanon in the context of the Arab Spring. I argued that the Lebanese women's movement has entered a fourth phase of heightened activism through the utilization of new media technologies, which enabled them to reach a wider audience for free and to self-publish and circulate their ideas. In so doing, they have been able to invert the flow of information from traditional media to new media sources and to become both the source and distributor of the message. The key message, however, is a new and more radical conceptualization of the source of women's oppression than previously identified in the first three phases of the Lebanese women's movement. The fourth phase of the Lebanese women's movement is an informal network of activists, following social movement theory, who have adopted an intersectional approach to the women's rights puzzle in Lebanon, which link's women's rights with civil rights. While a state of emergency can stall social progress, nonetheless, the online/ offline campaign to make domestic violence illegal in April 2014 succeeded in bringing about legislative change during a political deadlock. It might not be a panacea, but the legislative success demonstrates the dynamism of the online and offline modes of activism utilized by feminist activists in Lebanon today. We now turn in the next chapter to intersectional activism, which links women's rights with civil rights.

NOTES

1. See the *Guardian*: http://www.theguardian.com/global-development/2014/apr/09/lebanese-bill-domestic-violence-marital-rape.
2. See the *Guardian*: http://guardianlv.com/2013/12/arab-spring-turning-into-arab-winter-in-egypt/.
3. Women achieved the right to vote in Lebanon in 1953.
4. Women won the right to travel without the permission of their husband in 1974.

5. Contraception was legalized in Lebanon in 1983.

6. See the website of Nasawiya in Lebanon: http://www.nasawiya.org/web/about-us/what-is-feminism/.

7. This survey was conducted as part of this study in 2012, was distributed online via email, Facebook, and Linkedin and had 110 respondents.

8. See *Al Jazeera* in-depth feature article: http://www.aljazeera.com/indepth/features/2014/03/women-decry-lebanon-domestic-violence-law-2014327115352486894.html.

9. See *Al Akhbar*: http://english.al-akhbar.com/node/18945.

10. See *AFP on Yahoo News*: http://news.yahoo.com/lebanon-passes-law-against-domestic-violence-180739224.html.

11. See *BBC*, 2014 "Lebanon Protesters March over Domestic Violence. https://www.bbc.com/news/world-middle-east-26502445.

Chapter 5

Intersectional Activism

Civil Rights and Women's Rights

INTRODUCTION

This chapter discusses the intersection between the new wave of women's rights activism and broader social and political movements in Lebanon. The campaigns considered in this chapter overlap and address a broad array of social and political grievances that Lebanese have experienced with the state, or its absence. From women's nationality rights, to electoral reform, women's quotas in parliament, and the #YouStink garbage campaigns of 2015, the campaigns show the intersection between the women's rights deficit and the deadlock in Lebanon's political system and vice versa. This chapter starts by examining the campaign for women's nationality rights and then considers the movement for electoral reform and the debate on a women's quota in parliament, by examining the results of the 2018 election. The chapter concludes with a discussion of the political and ecological crisis, which arose out of Lebanon's garbage crisis in 2015, which led to more garbage washing up on Lebanon's shores in 2018. The chapter asks, can improving women's representation in parliament resolve the nationality question, reduce sectarianism, and fix the ecological crisis?

WOMEN'S NATIONALITY CAMPAIGN

Women's nationality rights, or their absence, is one of the key campaigns of the Lebanese women's movement, which seek to extend nationality rights to women, so they can pass nationality rights onto their children. The first question to ask is, why don't women have nationality rights in Lebanon? As noted in the introduction and chapter 3, women are considered to be "wards of their husbands," within both religious and civil law, with their roles mediated by significant male guardians, either the father or husband (Moghadam and Roudi-Fahimi 2005; Shehadeh 2010). While the system of male guardianship (*walayah*) is more comprehensive in Iran and Saudi Arabia, although somewhat amended in 2019,[1] the practice still operates to a less degree within Lebanon's civil and religious laws. The current nationality law, Decree No.15 1925, is structured on a patrilineal logic, whereby citizenship is inherited from a Lebanese father by descent, or by marriage to a Lebanese husband. Citizenship, therefore, is reckoned by patrilineal descent and follows the logic of religious affiliation, which also privileges the patrilineal family, over the individual woman, as the bearer and reproducer of the patrilineage. Indeed, the question of women's group membership is one of the contradictions of patrilineal logic, which traces property, religion, the custody of children, and citizenship through men but reproduces group members through women. Ironically, it is noted that women's second-class citizenship status was made worse during the French Mandate, when Decree No.15 was implemented, in which Article 1 stipulates that, to be Lebanese, one must be

> Born of a Lebanese father, born in Greater Lebanon and did not acquire foreign nationality upon birth or by affiliation and every person born in the greater Lebanon territory of unknown parents or parents of unknown nationality. (Decree No15 on Lebanese Nationality, January 19, 1925)

By contrast, under the previous Ottoman-era nationality law of the early 1800s, nationality could be inherited via bilineal descent from either the mother or the father. The legal principle, which changed between the two nationality laws, was a change from nationality being determined via relationship to land (*jus soli*), to nationality being determined via patrilineal descent, reckoned through blood ties to a Lebanese father (*jus sanguinis*) (Ghaddar 2017). A subsequent amendment to the Ottoman nationality law in 1869 prioritized blood over land. Under the 1925 nationality law, illegitimate children and "foreign" women married to Lebanese husbands have more rights than Lebanese women to nationality, as chapter 3 highlighted. Pateman (1988) argued, in Western contexts, that the sexual contract, based upon the conjugal marriage union, was central to the polity of the West, yet within the Lebanese context, sectarian collectivities mediate individual membership to the nation and the nature of the marriage contract. Moreover, as Charrad (2001) has noted, in Islamic family law the rights of the patrilineage are privileged over the conjugal family unit, a point also confirmed by Cuno (2015). Thus, in Lebanon, the rights of sects take precedence, through the conjugal union, and women follow their husband's nationality based on a patrilineal logic. However, the system also creates many legal loopholes and contradictions the most important of which is the future prospects of children born in Lebanon to Lebanese mothers and non-Lebanese fathers, who are officially "stateless."

Across the region, women's rights groups have attempted to reform family law, which in all countries, other than Tunisia and Turkey, is based on the *Shari'a* (Moghadam and Roudi-Fahimi 2005), while in Lebanon separate personal status codes apply to Christians and Muslims, as noted in chapter 3. However, the principle of patrilineality operates across Lebanon's eighteen recognized religious communities, including Muslims and non-Muslims. Joseph (1996b) notes that throughout the Middle East, women are subject to patriarchal structures and patrilineal ideologies, which privilege males and elders through kinship. Moreover, she argues that personal status laws, which regulate marriage, divorce, inheritance, and child custody, are the key mode by which Middle Eastern states incorporate subnational communities and religious sects into "juridical communities" and regulate women's sexuality to reproduce both sect and nation (Joseph 1996, 7). However, across the region there has been pressure to reform personal status and citizenship laws. Both Egypt and Algeria gave women the right to pass on citizenship in 2004 (Moghadam and Roudi-Fahimi 2005).

Activists must navigate a pathway between universal values and divergent sectarian practices in the case of Lebanon. Women's unequal nationality and citizenship rights form a core grievance with the Lebanese state. Full citizenship rights are only acquired through a woman's relationship with her father and then her husband[2] (CRTD.A/UNDP 2004), what Joseph (1996a, 9) refers to as "relational citizenship," as noted in chapters 1 and 2. If a woman is married to a non-Lebanese man, her children, subsequently, are denied citizenship. As Charafeddine (2009, 13) writes, nationality rights go to the heart of the confessional system in Lebanon:

> Under a sectarian political system that is established on the distribution of the spoils between confessions, numbers play a major role in determining these spoils and their future trends. . . . If the patriarchal Lebanese social system has set the foundations of discrimination against women in Lebanese laws early since its establishment, the sectarian political system has thwarted any possibility to amend these laws until now.

Therefore, women's nationality rights are central to both the reproduction and resolution of Lebanon's women's rights puzzle. However, restricting the nationality rights of Lebanese women also intentionally denies citizenship rights to Palestinian men, one of the largest refugee populations in Lebanon, as opponents fear a shift in the "sectarian balance" away from Christians to Muslims (Dorigo 2013). Sunni Palestinian men were estimated to constitute 38 percent of non-Lebanese husbands in Lebanon, according to a report written by the United Nations Development Program (UNDP) (Charafeddine 2009, 20). Thus, the acquisition of citizenship through marriage is restricted for non-Lebanese husbands but not for non-Lebanese wives, adding to the nationality rights double standard.

Hence, Lebanese women's nationality rights are shaped and constrained by the logic of sect and the perceived balance between the sects. The concept of "sectarian balance" (Ghaddar 2017) is a key justification for the maintenance of citizenship rights for Lebanese males only and the denial of nationality rights to Lebanese women. As there has not been a census in Lebanon since 1932, as noted in chapter 2, the relative proportion of each sect, to the overall population distribution, is not officially known, but it is commonly thought that Lebanese Christians now account for only 37 percent of the population (Economist 2016; Traboulsi 2012), as noted in the preface. The decline in the percentage of Christians was exacerbated by the civil war migrations, in which Christians outnumbered Muslims, and by the arrival of Palestinian and Syrian refugee populations into Lebanon with a Muslim majority. While the *Tai'f* accord revised the proportion of Christians to Muslims in parliament to parity, as noted in chapter 2, the Christian allocation of seats is disproportional to their demographic share of the population in modern Lebanon, hence their fear of decline into minority status, with a corresponding loss of representation in parliament. Consequently, women's citizenship rights are restricted to preserve the "sectarian balance" between Christians and Muslims, leaving women caught between sect and nation.

However, women's restricted nationality rights are not the only controversy regarding the distribution of citizenship rights. According to Ghaddar (2017), there is a perception that citizenship rights are distributed, via naturalization or by political decree, to the political allies of leading politicians, or to certain demographics, which will increase the Christian population of Lebanon and turn the tide against their decline. The Citizenship Law of 2015, led by the Free Patriotic Movement and the Lebanese Forces, to restore nationality rights to the diaspora, or the descendants of Lebanese-born overseas, where Christian emigrants constitute the majority, was considered by some quarters one such strategy (Ghaddar 2017). However, Lebanese women who are born in Lebanon have never been the primary recipients of such political reforms to extend citizenship rights, leaving them to take matters into their own hands.

The campaign to reform Lebanon's Nationality law, Decree No.15, dating back to 1925, which would grant Lebanese women full nationality rights, has been led by CRTD.A. Efforts have been made for two decades, but a concerted campaign took off from 2002 to 2003, when they commissioned a number of studies on the effects of the nationality rights problem on women married to non-Lebanese husbands.[3] In 2005 the campaign "My Nationality, A right for

Me and My Family," or the "Nationality Campaign," was launched (Ghaddar 2017). The organization has worked in partnership and in coalition with a range of organizations including Commission of the Status of Women, Equality Without Reservation, Women Learning Partnership, and regionally with organizations in Egypt, Bahrain, Morocco, and Algeria, through organizations such as the Association for Women's Rights and Development (Interview, Beirut 2013). The framework that CRTD.A follows for their work is guided by CEDAW, based on the concept of a universal human rights framework. A range of strategies have been deployed to reach audiences, including online strategies, as noted in chapter 4, such as email lists, social media, and websites. But the effectiveness of the online campaign in bringing about legislative change is questioned by the executive director of CRTD.A, who concludes,

> I think nothing can or should replace grass roots mobilization. You cannot have change and transformation without grass roots mobilization, without people taking interest taking action beyond clicking they have to go out and do something about it. (Interview, Beirut 2013)

Achieving grassroots mobilization has also encountered other hurdles. Competition for donor funding divided the campaign, for instance, when the UNDP announced funding for the nationality campaign and named the Committee for the Follow-up on Women's Issues (CFUWI) as their partner organization, not CRTD.A. Divisions over funding sources is a common narrative across the organizations of the Lebanese women's movement, as noted in chapter 4. The access to sponsorship, funding, and leadership from international organizations has been a divisive issue and, as occurred in the case of the Nationality Campaign in Lebanon, the UNDP was not in it for the long run and discontinued their funding after two years (Ghaddar 2017). As noted by one activist from CRTD.A, they have a selective policy of accepting external funding:

> [We] have a policy of not taking funding from specific governments and actually based on their position related to women. Basically, we try to fundraise from organizations that are known to have an agenda that supports women. (Interview, Beirut 2013)

The Nationality Campaign turned a corner in 2012 when a draft bill to review Article 4 of the 1925 Nationality Law came before the Lebanese Cabinet for consideration under the Mikati government. However, the committee advised the government against approving the amendment, because it would allow "foreigners" to gain Lebanese nationality. Legal cases were also put before the judiciary to test the case of Lebanese women married to non-Lebanese husbands. In both cases the strategy was, ultimately, rejected. However, the living conditions for the children of Lebanese women married to "foreign husbands" have been made easier, regarding accessing schooling and health care. The setback in the campaign for women's nationality rights followed the start of the civil war in Syria after 2011, when the women's movement again found their efforts for reform stymied by the broader regional and sectarian political machinations, which sought to maintain the status quo against the proposed changes (Ghaddar 2017).

While the movement, to date, has not achieved legislative change on women's nationality rights, the strategy is a long-term one, related to several key intersectional campaigns to bring about social change and gender justice in Lebanon, which cumulatively have made a difference. As noted in chapter 4, the Lebanese women's movement seeks to address four key interrelated campaigns: domestic violence law, women's nationality rights, women's quotas in parliament, and personal status law reform. Progress has been made on at least two key issues: a domestic violence law, as outlined in chapter 4, and the partial recognition of civil marriage, as the following chapter discusses. Yet many activists believe that no lasting legislative change will be achieved until women comprise a minimum proportion of seats in parliament, in order to bring about legal reform from within the legislature.

A WOMEN'S QUOTA IN PARLIAMENT?

The third key campaign of the Lebanese women's movement has been a concerted strategy to improve the representation of Lebanese women in parliament. While the Arab region, as a whole, has one of the lowest proportions of women in parliament in the world at 16 percent, in recent years many Arab countries have adopted gender quotas to reverse the trend (Dahelrup 2009). Lebanon, however, was ranked 122nd in the world in 2009 for the proportion of women in elected public office (El-Makari 2009, 39) and, subsequently, declined further to position 183 out of 193 countries in 2019 (IPU 2019). Nonetheless, the most recent election in 2018 saw six women elected into parliament in May 2018, representing 4.7 percent of the 128-member legislative body.[4] This was an improvement on the previous parliament, formed in 2009, which had only four women elected. In the 2018 election women made up 50.8 percent of the registered voters (UNDP 2018a). Overall, women comprised 14 percent of the candidates who ran for office, a total of 86 candidates out of 597, up from comprising only 1.9 percent of candidates in the 2009 election, 12 out of 702 candidates (UNDP 2018a). While this is an improvement, Lebanon still falls short in the region, and globally, in women's representation. The question is why?

Women are underrepresented in politics globally, with the average number of seats in world parliaments, occupied by women, being 19 percent in 2009 (Dahelrup 2009). Over the next decade that number increased to 23.6 percent, according to the Inter-Parliamentary Union (World Bank 2017). However, the reason for their absence rests not so much on the women themselves, or their lack of resources, but on the androcentric bias of political parties (UNDP 2018a), which leads to male-dominated party rooms, according to Krook (2009). Yet, women's representation has been improving globally, largely based on the adoption of gender quotas, including in Arab countries. In 1990 only twenty countries had adopted gender quotas, and by 2000 that number had increased to more than sixty (Krook 2009). Since the 1995 Beijing Platform for Action, women's rights activists around the world have called for a controversial 30 percent women's quota to redress the low representation of women in government and force social change using the "fast track model" (Dahelrup 2009, 30). In sub-Saharan Africa, Rwanda has become the country with the largest proportion of women in parliament, with a total of 53 percent of the parliamentary seats held by women, while the Scandinavian countries have an average female representation of 42 percent. Globally the rate in 2017 was 23.6 percent. The Middle Eastern region, however, has one of the lowest rates of women's political participation, with an average rate of only 16 percent in 2017, despite an increase from an average of 4 percent since 1990, according to the World Bank (2017). As of 2013, according to the Inter Parliamentary Union (IPU 2019), Saudi Arabia permits women to vote and serve in municipal elections and has a 20 percent women's quota.[5] The Pacific remains the region with the lowest rate of female representation in the world, with an average rate of 7 percent (World Bank 2017).

How can the trend be reversed? According to many scholars, gender quotas are the key to improving women's representation in politics, yet there are different approaches to implementing gender quotas. The first kind of gender quota is to reserve the number of seats in parliament for women and the second kind of quota is legislated candidate quotas. It has been found that women do better, overall, in a proportional representation system, while there are positives and negatives of each kind of quota system. Political parties, for instance, can place women in unwinnable seats on candidate lists. Nonetheless, all the countries, which have improved the representation of women in politics, have adopted a quota system, leading to the question, can women's representation improve the process of democratization overall? Importantly, Moghadam (2009) concludes that a critical mass is important for women's representation to make any substantial difference to the dynamics of power and political leadership. Women need to be at least a substantial minority in parliament, before an impact is made and women's issues receive more support (Moghadam 2009). Hence, the Beijing Platform for Action set the benchmark of 30 percent representation for the women's quota. While some countries have achieved a higher representation than the benchmark without a quota, notably Finland, with a female representation of 42 percent, as noted earlier, other developed countries remain stubbornly poor in their female representation, such as the United States, with a female representation of only 19 percent, while Argentina has achieved a female representation of 35 percent, on the strength of a gender quota (IPU 2019). Moghadam (2009) argues that the development of democracy and improving the participation and representation of women in government are intertwined processes as feminists have led the movements for democratic change. As is the case in Lebanon, women's rights activists are mindful of the need for sustainable democracies, otherwise institutionally weak democracies can have stakeholders who come to power and institute laws, which allocated women second-class citizenship status. Lastly, a democratic system, without women's human rights and gender equality can become a "male democracy" (Moghadam 2009).

But not everyone agrees that a women's quota is a panacea to cure all ills in the democratic process, or to improve women's status and position in society in Lebanon. Although Lebanon's National Commission on Parliamentary Electoral Law Reform, established by decree in 2005, included a gender quota for women in national elections, one has yet to be implemented. Further, Article, 64 made it an obligation for electoral lists in all districts to include women under a proportional voting system (El-Makari 2009). Additionally, in 2010 a law was proposed to ensure that 20 percent of municipal council seats were held by women, which still awaits approval (El-Helou 2009). One of the arguments, in the case of Lebanon, as to why there is ongoing resistance to the adoption of gender quotas, is that there is a long tradition of "women in black" serving in the Lebanese parliament, who are the wives of elites, or of former serving politicians who have died, as noted by Laure Moghaizel (cited in El-Makari 2009). Hence, female political representation has traditionally been the domain of elite women (Stephan 2019; El-Makari 2009). Second, there is a fear that gender quotas will only serve to reinforce the perception that women lack merit and can only gain representation through imposition (El-Makari 2009). Third, there is the view that Lebanon's system of confessional democracy is already constrained by a "sectarian quota" system, which makes forming governments increasingly protracted, resulting in repeated deadlocks and impasses, or absent posts, as was the case with the presidency between 2015 and 2017, as outlined in chapter 2. It is concluded by critics that adding a women's quota will only be an additional layer to an already prolonged and complex electoral process, which will be unworkable, as El-Helou notes:

> The division of the already confessionally distributed parliamentary seats between large and small electoral districts decreases the share of each sect in each district. This will inevitably increase the intensity of the electoral battle in the small districts, thus, decreasing, if not eliminating, the chances of women

and minorities in winning the competition, considering the traditional, feudal, sectarian, or familial powers are usually represented by "male candidates" capable of ensuring victory in tough battles. (El-Helou 2009, 60)

Similarly, El-Makari (2009) notes that the idea of a sectarian quota already forms the "core" of the Lebanese polity and culture, and a gender quota will act as a "new quota," on top of the existing sectarian and regional quotas, which form the core of the system of confessional democracy in Lebanon. As such, a women's quota will only be a burden for voters and an additional constraint on their electoral choices, according to the critics. Consequently, it creates a contradiction for the Lebanese consociational system, which works on the basis of a proportional power-sharing arrangement between sects (El-Makari 2009). Hence, an expansion of the representation of women works at odds with the structure of the confessional system and, thus, requires a reworking of the electoral law if it is to be successful in the future. Finally, a key argument against a gender quota is that it goes against the principle of equality. Rather, it breaches the principle of equal merit, to provide preferential treatment to women, in order to improve gender equity.

Despite the critics, activists still view a women's quota as a way forward to bring about legislative change. As outlined in chapter 4, the online survey of social media and women's rights issues (2012) found that the implementation of women's electoral quotas ranked sixth out of nine key issues identified, with citizenship and nationality law reform ranking first, anti-domestic violence legislation ranked equally with citizenship and nationality law reform, followed by personal status code law reform, the introduction of civil marriage, and inheritance laws. Yet the issues remain interconnected; without the reform of nationality and family law, women are unable to gain full citizenship rights, yet it remains difficult to introduce these law reforms when the representation of women in parliament remains only 4.7 percent, as was the outcome of Lebanon's 2018 parliamentary election, as noted earlier. Moreover, women need to be part of the decision-making and legislative process. Yet, it is difficult for women to improve their participation without a quota to reverse business as usual in the selection and election of candidates into Lebanon's parliament. As such, the implementation of a gender quota is a conundrum, without one woman's representation remains stubbornly low and, consequently, it continues to be difficult to introduce legislation to improve gender equality or implement a gender quota at all. One activist, who responded to the online survey, outlined a strategy to protest the poor representation of women in Lebanon's 2012 cabinet, which did not include any women:

Women's Quota organized a protest against absenting women from the last cabinet, where we asked people locally & internationally to stop any act or deed at 12:00 noon for 5 minutes as a protest. We required that those driving stop

their cars & blow their cars' horns also for five minutes. We used social media
& personal connections. It was a successful move. (Text response, online social
media and women's rights survey 2012)

While only a symbolic protest, nonetheless, it demonstrated the lack of satis-
faction with the status quo and the slow progress in improving women's representation in government in Lebanon. Indeed, women gained the right to vote
in Lebanon in 1952, but it wasn't until 2004 that the first-ever women ministers were appointed to the Lebanese parliament. The 2009 parliament had 2
women ministers and 4 women out of 128 were MPs, yet the cabinet had no
women at all (Khraiche 2012). One suggestion to overcome the problem was
to form a female political party to push for change. While the idea was supported by activists from *Nasawiya*, who argued that concerted political action
is needed to bring about change from within the political process. Others were
less convinced, including activists from the Committee for Women's Political
Empowerment, due to the inherently clientelist nature of Lebanese politics,
which is focused on personality cults and patronage (Khraiche 2012).

The question then becomes, how can women improve their representation
in government when the political process is skewed against their participation? The director of CRTD.A, when interviewed as part of this study in 2013,
noted the vicious cycle, and argued that systemic reform of the electoral system, as a whole, will be necessary to make any significant change, including
the adoption of a single electoral district with a women's quota. Moreover,
the question of secularism becomes a prominent point, which can make an
overarching difference to the political process, according to CRTD.A:

> We are an organization that works for a secular state. Only a secular state
> actually can guarantee freedom of belief for everybody, not a religious state.
> A religious state does not guarantee freedom of belief for everybody. It does
> not guarantee freedom of belief for the minorities, only a secular state respects
> freedom of belief. (Interview, Beirut 2013)

Thus, women's electoral reform is considered integral to the reform of
Lebanon's consociational voting system, moving it toward secularism. Yet,
a single electoral district was not achieved, sectarian quotas remain, and a
women's quota was never implemented, despite the reform of Lebanon's
electoral law in 2017, for the Lebanese parliamentary elections, which finally
took place on May 6, 2018. Two different voting laws were considered: an
Orthodox Law, which was majoritarian, and a Proportional Voting Law.
Eventually the Proportional Voting Law prevailed over the old sectarian
law dating back to 1960 and was adopted in 2017 by the Aoun government
for the first time in Lebanese history.[6] While it did not end the confessional
system, as seats were still reserved by sect, voters, regardless of sect, could

vote for all seats in their district, based on a list, and preferential votes were also counted. The candidate with the highest number of votes, within each religious confession, was elected.[7] The total number of districts was reduced from 26 to 15, each with minor districts, and the confessional distribution was maintained, with parity between Muslims and Christians across 128 seats, as noted in chapter 2. Additionally, the Lebanese diaspora was permitted to vote, as nationality law and suffrage were extended to the diaspora, based on patrilineal descent to a Lebanese grandfather, as noted earlier in this chapter. Also, the new voting law was criticized for not including a women's quota, hence the logic of sectarian balance prevailed over gender equity.

Women, consequently, have only barely scratched the surface of Lebanese politics, which needs to level the playing field for women if significant change is to take place (Najjar 2018). While the 2018 election, the first in almost a decade, saw eighty-six women run as candidates, or 14.4 percent overall, after encouragement from Jean Ogasapian, the first women's affair's minister, whose appointment was not without controversy.[8] He had hoped to have at least five times more women elected to parliament. A billboard campaign was run in the Lebanese capital, titled "Half the society, half the Parliament," funded by the EU and the United Nations (Deeb 2018). Yet, the final outcome fell well short of expectations. Nonetheless, women did extend their representation in parliament to six seats, from four seats in 2009, which was an improvement (UNDP 2018; Deeb 2018).

It was surmised that even with the greater participation of women on the candidate lists for the election, brought about by the move to proportional voting, they were placed on minority, noncompetitive seats, due to male domination in the selection process (Najjar 2018). Indeed, the question of a women's quota was not even discussed when the government debated the new electoral law in 2017, with Hezbollah refusing to endorse it and arguing that the role of lawmaker is not "befitting for a woman in Lebanon," as "she has a home, she is a mother and must bring up [future] generations" (Deeb 2018). The problem of improving women's representation in parliament is compounded by the sectarian system, which mixes sect and patriarchy, resulting in the male domination of political institutions. Activists argue that women need to change the nature of political institutions, in order to break out of the mold of male-dominated politics as usual, with leading families from key religious sects and legacy political parties, which view adding women to their lists as adding "decorative women" only (Osseiran 2018). Indeed, the director of CRTD.A notes,

> It's time for Lebanon to go passed conservatism, to go passed patriarchy, to go passed a confessional system, because as long as we're in this horrible patriarchal and corrupt system we're not going to be able to move forward. (Interview, Beirut 2013)

Notwithstanding the potential limitations of women's quotas, the link between widening women's political participation and passing progressive laws, which improve gender equity, is an important precedent, which has occurred in other countries in the region. As Moghadam (2009) surmises, women need to reach a minimum critical mass, before legislative change becomes possible in parliament. For example, the increased proportion of women in parliament in Morocco was part of a successful reform process, which led to the ratification of an amended personal status code or family law, known as the *Moudawana*, by Morocco's parliament in 2004, which started a social revolution in family matters, by enhancing women's marriage, divorce, and alimony rights (Zoglin 2009). The process, which led to the reform of the family law system, started with the adoption of a National Plan for the Integration of Women in Development, put forward by King Mohammed the VI in 1999 (Zoglin 2009, 967). Subsequently, an important factor in passing the significant reforms to the personal status code in 2004 was the adoption of a gender quota for women in parliament in 2002, which reserved 30 out of 325, or 9 percent, of seats in the Chamber of Representatives for women, via a national list for elections in Morocco (Liddell 2009). Over time, the proportion of women in parliament rose to be one of the highest in the Arab region, 9 percent, and led to a broader acceptance of women in public life and the appointment of women to other leadership positions in the judiciary and as senior advisors (Liddell 2009).

Yet, scholars have noted, embedding women's progress within state structures does have potential drawbacks, as the feminist agenda might lose its autonomy or turn into "state feminism" and, therefore, become beholden to authoritarian or clientelist networks and power structures (Moghadam 2009). Also, elite women, more generally, are better placed to stand for nomination to the parliament under a quota system, a phenomenon Lebanese politics is long familiar with, as noted in the "women in black" trope, and the history of campaigners from the intellectual class and the *haute bourgeoisie*, using their *mahsoubieh*, or kinship capital, to bring about change and improve women's representation (Stephan 2019). While a women's quota is put forward as a potential solution, the quotidian problem of gender-based violence is all too real, as an interview with an activist from ABAAD highlighted in 2012:

> I think there is a common calculator when it comes to issues of discrimination and violence against women per se. Even with laws, or with policies, it is always the same. A women's quota—[won't make a] difference. . . . If you have a law for a quota and political participation rights, women will continue to suffer from issues related to gender-based violence. (Interview, Beirut 2012)

One of the cyclical arguments about the advancement of women's rights in Lebanon is that the struggle regularly becomes eclipsed by other more pressing national crises. Instead, the campaign is placed on the backburner, while the political focus switches to other more immediate problems. In 2015, the key problem that could not be ignored was the stench of garbage and rubbish, which built up on the streets of Beirut, due to the failure of municipal authorities to process Lebanon's rubbish, which became emblematic of all that was wrong with the Lebanese polity.

#YOUSTINK AND POLITICAL ECOLOGICAL STRUGGLES

The closure of Beirut's main landfill in the Naameh district, in July 2015, was the start of the garbage crisis, as residents blocked waste collectors from accessing the site, because it was close to homes and the government had failed to find an alternative landfill site, despite repeated requests. As no alternative site was found, in the short term, rubbish stockpiled on the city streets, health hazards developed from polluted air and groundwater and, ultimately, resulted in an enduring political, social, and ecological crisis. By July 17, 2015, 2,500 tons of garbage per day piled up on the streets, in rivers and, eventually, on beaches in and around Beirut.

A digitally switched on, youth-led movement, quickly filled the void and demanded action to address the waste management crisis, including consideration of everyday practices. The nature of political power and the confessional system in Lebanon was held responsible for the protracted political crisis, due to a lack of accountability and endemic corruption.[9] The online/offline social movement #YouStink took the lead in demanding action to resolve the crisis, and the social and political system, which produced it (Kraidy 2016; Khalil 2017; Abi Yaghi et al. 2017). Garbage piling up in the streets of Beirut and neighboring towns soon became the symbol of all that was wrong with the political system in Lebanon, which laid bare the incompetence of government processes and procedures (Khalil 2017). Something had to be done to put pressure on the government to act and find a long-term solution to the crisis, which included sustainable recycling, as the group's mission statement explains:

> #YouStink is a Lebanese grassroots movement created as a response to the government's inability to solve the ongoing trash crisis in a sustainable way. We are pushing for sustainable solutions provided by several environmental experts and centred around going back to a municipality-level system, while implementing nationwide recycling. (in Khalil 2017, 706)

Key demands were broader than a single issue, or what might be termed a NIMBY campaign (not in my backyard), and soon linked to longer-term grievances with the Lebanese political system. The key demands of the #YouStink movement included the resignation of the environment minister, a sustainable waste management strategy, parliamentary elections, and tackling corruption in the political class. Street protests began, and social media-led online/offline strategies were also deployed. Initially the government was given forty-eight hours to meet their demands or the street protests would resume (Kraidy 2016). An array of organizations and cross-sectoral actors became involved in the campaign to propose and develop alternative solutions, where the government was "missing in action."

While the civil war ended in 1990, effective public administration has remained a low priority, as protracted political crises, impasses, and vacancies in the executive branch take up the available oxygen, leaving the trivial matter of "who takes out the garbage" overlooked, due to more pressing crises. The consequences were significant. Within a week of the garbage crisis commencing, 22,000 tons of garbage had piled up on the streets and, combined with hot weather, it soon symbolized the unbearable stench of the "body politic" (Kraidy 2016). As noted in chapter 2, by the time the garbage crisis hit in Lebanon, they were in the second year of a protracted political crisis, in which the government was in a state of paralysis and dysfunction, with the presidency left vacant, due to the end of Michael Sleiman's term, and the postponement of parliamentary elections, leaving a caretaker government in charge. For activists, the garbage crisis exposed the government to be a "decomposing corpse" (Kraidy 2016, 21).

Moreover, the impact of the garbage crisis on human health has been well documented, from the impact of garbage handling on the workers themselves (Morsi et al. 2017), to the impact of burning Lebanon's waste on air quality, which led people to "inhale their death" (Human Rights Watch 2017). Studies have also found a link between waste-related pollution and incidences of cancer in Lebanon (Azar and Azar 2016). However, the accumulation of unprocessed rubbish also led to an environmental crisis for waterways and beaches, as much of the rubbish found its way into the sea and then returned to shore.

A series of failed government initiatives were implemented to resolve the crisis in 2015 and none of them went ahead. These included attempting to open a new landfill, but considerable opposition existed to this option from the municipalities and civil society (Massena 2016). A second strategy the government attempted was to export the waste by ship overseas, announced on December 21, 2015. Two companies were approached, Howa BV from the Netherlands and Chinook Urban Mining International of the United Kingdom (Kohn 2016). In the first instance, the plan was to export the waste to Russia, which ultimately was canceled by the British firm commissioned to lead the undertaking, as they had failed to obtain the relevant documents that proved Russia had agreed to accept the waste (Barrington 2016). Moreover, an alternative plan to export the waste to sub-Saharan Africa by ship also failed, due to corruption allegations and failure by the government and the contracted company to sign the relevant agreements. It seems that government ministers were misled into the deal to ship the rubbish to Sierra Leone, which activists allege was illegal under the Basal Convention, ratified by Lebanon in 1994 (Kodeih et al. 2016). Sierra Leone, subsequently, canceled the deal. What is more, Lebanon's rubbish would be costly to export, as it was unprocessed and had been piling up for many months. The government, consequently, was forced back to considering landfill and incineration to process the garbage, despite the health risks associated with this course of action (Barrington 2016).

Despite street protests numbering some 200,000 people, calling for a long-term solution, illegally dumped rubbish found its way into the sea (Jay and Russell 2017). "Out of sight, is out of mind" became the short-term strategy, given the ongoing government paralysis, while no long-term strategy was prioritized. However, two years later the rubbish that was dumped into the sea washed back up on Lebanese shores, following winter storms in January 2018 (Wedeman 2018). Moreover, repeated winter storms, brought further rubbish to Lebanon's shorelines, resulting in multiple attempts to clean beaches, such as on the banks of the River Kalb, north of Beirut (Wedeman 2018). Once known for its beautiful beaches and scenery, the garbage washing ashore was not the image Lebanon wanted to project to the world. Initially, relying on volunteers to clean the beaches, the closed public beaches drew attention to the fact that the problem was not going away any time soon. Soon the ecological crisis turned into an economic crisis, as the garbage crisis had a negative impact on the tourism industry, with summer approaching. Zouk Mosbeh, a beach at the epicenter of the crisis, hosts many resorts that are popular in the summer, instead, they were surrounded by rotting piles of rubbish that had already been washed ashore more than sixteen times (Galer 2018).

Alternative solutions were sought that bypassed government processes and relied on citizen action. The group Recycle Lebanon was formed to coordinate volunteers to clean up the coastal rubbish. It was founded by Kazak in 2014 to tackle environmentally friendly waste disposal and recycling (Kohn 2016). However, Lebanon continues to generate 7,000 tons of rubbish per day and 50 percent of it is thrown into landfills, while the main company, Sukleen, recycles only 9 percent of what it collects (Fawaz 2018). Hence, rubbish continues to be directly dumped into the sea, or into coastal landfills, where it quickly finds its way into the sea, which is an ongoing disaster for the shoreline and public health (Galer 2018).

The environmental engineer Ziad Abi Chaker rejects incineration as a viable solution to the rubbish, because of the air pollution it creates. Moreover, it has been found that Lebanon's waste contains 70 percent organic material, which is too wet for the incineration process, if it is left unsorted (Galer 2018). He operates Cedar Environmental, which provides composting facilities and a glass recycling plant, plus the manufacture of Eco-Board, as part of a longer-term solution to Lebanon's garbage (Fawaz 2018). New recycling infrastructure to sort the rubbish is needed, leading to employment opportunities in Lebanon, but it also offers an alternative to the throwaway culture in Lebanon. Much of the rubbish contains single-use plastics, disposable coffee cups, medical waste, and hookah pipes. It is estimated that Lebanon needs thirty-five recycling factories to tackle the scale of Lebanon's daily garbage and to start moving toward the circular economy (Fawaz 2018).

Like other social movements, Lebanon's garbage movement soon led to broader intersectional calls to address the sectarian system itself, echoing the call of the Arab Spring, *ash sha'ab yurid isqat an-nizam* (the people want the fall of the regime). The key grievances also broadened to include government accountability, effective public administration, transparency, social justice, and, ultimately, an *'almani* (secular) system of government. For even the garbage had taken on a sectarian (*ta'ifa*) flavor, with the confessionalization of garbage collection and distribution put forward as one solution to the crisis. Confessional garbage became a "thing" and a trending Internet meme, with one joke referring to "Shi'ite garbage bags in Achrafieh," a Christian neighborhood in Beirut (Abi Yaghi et al. 2017). If rubbish had become a sectarian issue, resolving the garbage crisis involved more than simply picking up the rubbish; the structural and political dimensions also had to be addressed.

Moreover, a common viewpoint is that the garbage problem is emblematic of the chronic problems besetting Lebanon's political system, leading to protracted bouts of political paralysis. Another such political crisis embroiled Lebanon following the May 2018 election, with no cabinet being formed until February 2019. While the garbage crisis started from a single issue, it soon expanded into a broader movement to address the intersecting causes of Lebanon's political impasses, lack of governance, corruption, and inaction. Indeed, garbage crises have occurred elsewhere and grown into major social movements, such as Chicago's garbage wars, India's garbage crisis (Doron and Jeffrey 2018), and now the United States and Australia are facing recycling problems, since China no longer will import low-quality recycling waste for their incinerator plants. In the meantime, Lebanon's garbage crisis is certain to return, while the chronic state of political paralysis and lack of governance continues in Lebanon, as the uprising of October 2019 highlights.

CONCLUSION

This chapter examined the intersection between women's rights campaigns and the broader social and political movements that have emerged in Lebanon since 2015. Three key campaigns were examined, which address a broad array of social and political grievances that Lebanese have experienced with the state, or its absence. From women's nationality rights, to electoral reform and women's quotas, to the #YouStink garbage movement, the campaigns show the intersection between the women's rights deficit, the lack of effective governance, and the quest for secular solutions to the sectarian deadlock at the core of Lebanon's political system. The chapter examined the links between these seemingly disparate campaigns, which aim to expand women's nationality rights and representation in government, as well as redress the ecological crisis that has arisen out of rubbish left uncollected in the streets. The interrelated women's rights and civil society campaigns were examined for their contemporary salience and the multifaceted characteristics of Lebanese social movements in the contemporary era. In each case, it is evident that improving women's nationality rights, gender justice, and the representation of women in politics will improve governance, but such reforms are limited by the sectarian structure of the legal and political system. On the one hand, each campaign examined in this chapter was hindered by a confessional logic, whether it be the women's nationality campaign, the women's quota in parliament, or the garbage crisis. On the other hand, each identified grievance remained unresolved, as such, because the alternative would alter the current sectarian balance and, in turn, the confessional system as a whole, so the status quo continues. The next chapter will examine Lebanon's civil marriage campaign and the implications for women's rights, civil rights, and the confessional system.

NOTES

1. There is a view that Saudi Arabia amended its male guardianship system due to international pressure.

2. Nationality rights are patrilineal and pass through the male line.

3. See Ziad Baroud, https://nationalitycampaign.wordpress.com/2010/03/13/zi ad-baroud-womens-right-to-nationality/.

4. See the *New Arab*, "Six Lebanese Women Voted in Parliament," May 8, 2018, https://www.alaraby.co.uk/english/news/2018/5/8/the-six-lebanese-women-voted-int o-parliament.

5. This move was cynically viewed by some commentators as a token gesture to improve Saudi Arabia's standing in the international community, without making a great deal of difference.

6. See https://gulfnews.com/opinion/editorials/lebanon-passing-parliamentary-law-is-a-step-in-right-direction-1.2044624.

7. See http://www.naharnet.com/stories/en/245764 and https://www.newyorker.com/news/news-desk/is-lebanons-new-electoral-system-a-path-out-of-sectarianism.

8. See article by Timour Azhari, "Women's Minister Says Being Male a 'positive,'" *Daily Star* October 29, 2018, https://www.pressreader.com/.

9. Lebanon is ranked 138/180 countries, according to the 2019 Corruption Perceptions Index, reported by *Transparency International*; see https://www.transparency.org/country/LBN. Contributing factors include conflict of interests among public officials and illicit enrichments.

Chapter 6

The Quest for Civil Marriage

INTRODUCTION

This chapter considers the movement for civil marriage reform as part of the Lebanese women's movement's campaign for comprehensive personal status law reform and the adoption of a unified civil status code. In the previous chapter I considered the intersection between the Lebanese women's movement and civil society campaigns for women's nationality rights, reform of the voting system, including women's electoral representation, and improved public administration, or its absence, in the garbage crisis. This chapter considers perhaps the most contentious issue facing women's rights in Lebanon, the reform of personal status law, as embodied in the civil marriage debate in Lebanon. The debate raises important questions regarding the location of women between sect and nation in Lebanon, due to the absence of a civil marriage law and differential personal status codes, as outlined in chapter 3, for all matters relating to marriage, divorce, maintenance, inheritance, and child custody. While it is not the first time a civil marriage law has been introduced in Lebanon, the recognition of Lebanon's first civil marriage in 2013 reignited the national debate, as a new generation of activists sought the recognition of civil marriage before the courts. This chapter starts by defining civil marriage in the Lebanese context; it then examines the argument for civil marriage by analyzing the motivations of three case study civil marriage couples. The argument against the recognition of civil marriage is then considered. The chapter concludes with a consideration of the implications of the civil marriage debate for the women's rights puzzle in Lebanon.

WHAT IS CIVIL MARRIAGE?

A civil marriage is defined as "a wedding that takes place without any religious affiliation, outside of a religious court or place of worship, is usually performed by a government official or a civil celebrant, and is based upon a civil contract and a civil marriage law."[1] Lebanon currently has no civil marriage law,[2] despite an intervention during the French Mandate to unify Lebanon's personal status codes in 1936 under a law referred to as 60LR (Assaf 2009), as outlined in chapter 3. There have been eight subsequent attempts to introduce a civil marriage law in Lebanon since 1951, when the Lebanese Bar Association went on strike for six months to demand an optional civil marriage law. Another attempt was made to introduce a civil marriage law in 1957, by MP Raymond Edde, as well as in 1972 by the Democratic Party, in 1976 by the National Movement, in 1977 by the Syrian Socialist National Party, and again in 1998 by President Elias Hrawi. In 2011 the Chaml Association, and fourteen other women's rights and civil society organizations put up a draft civil marriage law that was never debated before the parliament, because of the depth of clerical opposition to the reform. Finally, Minister of Justice Chakib Kortbawi submitted a bill to the cabinet to grant the right for optional civil marriage, without removing one's religious affiliation from civil records in 2014, but it was criticized for allowing funds to be paid directly to the religious court of the husband's family (Human Rights Watch 2015).

In the absence of a civil marriage law in Lebanon, couples seeking a civil marriage have resorted to the "Cyprus solution," whereby a civil marriage is contracted outside of Lebanon, where there are civil marriage tourism industries servicing Lebanese couples.[3] Most commonly is Cyprus, where couples marry under the Cypriot civil marriage law, or in Turkey under a Turkish civil marriage law. The number of couples who contracted a civil marriage in Cyprus increased from 220 in 2008 to 700 in 2011.[4,5] Moreover, a civil marriage costs considerably less than a religious wedding in Lebanon, because there are fewer guests and "fanfare" and no fees for the services of a priest or *sheikh*. What is more, some couples do not invite their family at all, as we will see later in the chapter. Hence the lower cost of a civil marriage is considered an advantage by the couples themselves, when weddings in Lebanon are costly, have many guests, and often require a bank loan. With the average wedding in Lebanon costing 50,000 USD, and sometimes considerably more, a civil marriage package in Cyprus, according to Nadia Travel, a specialist tourism agency specializing in civil marriages, costs only 950 USD per person, or 1900 USD for a package.[6] With a financial crisis and high unemployment rates in Lebanon, the lower cost is attractive to couples who are keen not to go into debt. Has the time come for Lebanon to adopt a civil marriage law?

THE ARGUMENT FOR CIVIL
MARRIAGE LAW REFORM

The first civil marriage contracted on Lebanese soil in 2013 reignited the national debate (The Daily Star 2013a, b, c, e). The couple were both Muslims, one Shi'ite, the other Sunni. They chose to utilize the old French Mandate 60LR[7] civil law, with the help of a notary and a decree dating from 2007 that allows citizens to remove their religious affiliation from their administrative record. While the then president supported the move, the then prime minister and prominent religious clerics, including the Grand Mufti of Lebanon, Mohammad Rashid Qabbani, opposed it (The Daily Star 2013b). Meanwhile, protesters in support of civil marriage carried signs at a protest in downtown Beirut, reading, "civil marriage, not civil war" (Maroun 2013). A supporter of civil marriage explains why they support the reform:

> I support civil marriage, because the laws in Lebanon are sectarian ones in which the Lebanese people are distributed amongst their sects or religions and each sect follows its role. This has created a very big problem between people and conflict. You cannot marry from other sects, you can't live with other sects and sometimes you can't rent a house in a different sects' region. For this reason, we support a civil law, because we need to live together due to all these conflicts in Lebanon. It is a door. The civil marriage deprives the religious people from their authority and their economic situation, because it deprives them of the money they are going to take from the Church or Mosque or the religious court, and second, it will deprive them from the authority over people. Political people are also against civil marriage, because they also practice their authority over people in a sectarian way. And the civil marriage and civil law stops them from being afraid of each other and living in different confederacies in Lebanon. (Interview, Beirut 2013)

As can be seen in this interview excerpt, the arguments for civil marriage are based on, first, the ability to facilitate interaction between sects and, second, removing the power and authority from religious institutions to govern marriage.

However, the civil marriage debate is not without controversy. Amid significant media coverage and public debate, the then minister of the interior, Charbel, ratified the first civil marriage contracted on Lebanese soil under the old French law, 60LR, on April 23, 2013. Since the recognition of the landmark civil marriage in Lebanon in 2013, fifty more civil marriages were contracted under the same law, but the subsequent minister of the interior declined to ratify the marriages, at the time of writing, and referred them to the civil court for adjudication (The Daily Star 2013e). Another prominent civil marriage took place in Lebanon in June 2019, which also awaits ratification by the interior minister, setting a further precedent for change.[8]

Meanwhile, a 2014 draft civil marriage law still awaits final ratification before the parliament, despite frequent street protests throughout 2014 and 2015 in support of the reform. A series of mass rallies were held in Beirut in 2015 calling for secularism, civil marriage rights, and women's rights.[9] As KAFA outlines, civil marriage is very much a civil right, according to advocates, because:

> The state in Lebanon contravenes what is stated in the introduction of its constitution and its international obligations, because rather than passing a fair public law that equalizes between individuals in their rights and responsibilities and brings them together under one modern law, it has reinforced community and sectarian divisions by subjecting them to 15 different sectarian laws, the only similarity between them is their regression, sexism and discrimination against women. (KAFA 2019)

However, as the impasse continues between advocates and opponents, the debate comes back to the same controversial sticking point: the introduction of civil marriage would shift the jurisdiction of marriage from religious to civil law and, hence, it is seen as the first step toward dismantling the confessional system. El-Cheikh (1998, 156) similarly found, in a 1998 study, of the opposition to civil marriage reform that:

> The introduction of the optional civil law was understood by many, both opponents and supporters, as the first battle for the progressive dismantling of the confessional system, but the activists pushing for the civil marriage bill soon came to regret the association of the two issues.

Given the controversy surrounding civil marriages and the perceived link between the introduction of civil marriage and the dismantling of confessionalism in Lebanon, this study investigated why both civil rights and women's rights activists support civil marriage law reform and why there is opposition to such a change in Lebanon, as outlined in the methods section in chapter 1. The online survey of civil marriage attitudes (2013),[10] conducted in the second phase of this study, found a high level of support among respondents for the reform of personal status codes in Lebanon, with 98 percent supporting a unified civil status code for Lebanon (see figure 6.1) and 98 percent of respondents to the online survey supporting civil marriage reform (see figure 6.2).

Respondents were then asked why they supported civil marriage reform and what were the advantages of civil marriage. According to one respondent, it can "protect personal freedoms and open relationships between persons of different communities." Intermarriage, across sectarian lines, is put forward

Should a unified civil status code be introduced in Lebanon?

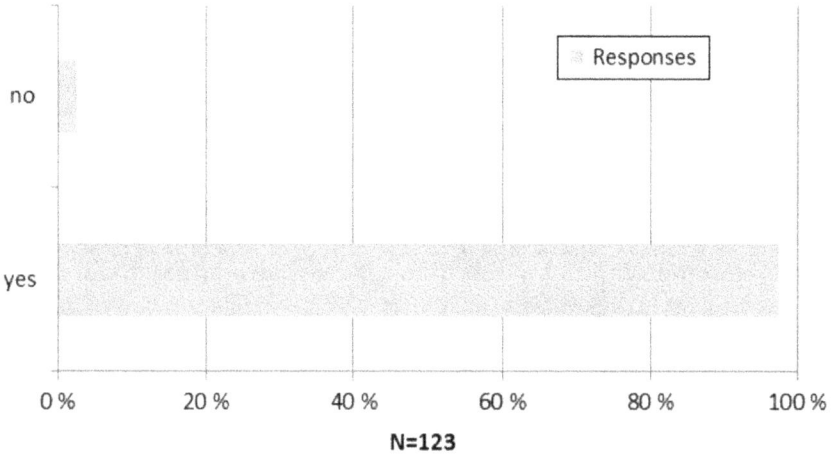

Figure 6.1 **Support for Unified Civil Status Code.** *Source*: Online survey of civil marriage attitudes 2013.

Do you support the introduction of civil marriage in Lebanon?

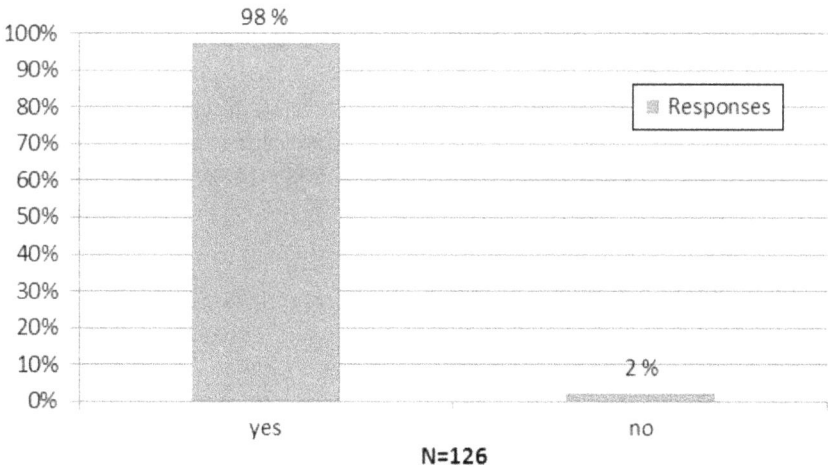

Figure 6.2 **Support for Civil Marriage.** *Source*: Online survey of civil marriage attitudes.

as an advantage, which can build bridges in a society divided along sectarian lines, as this respondent explains:

> People will mix with other religions, will respect others more and they will stop talking sectarianism. A woman will have the right to divorce if she is unhappy, she will have the right to give her family name to her children, she will be able to register him/her and most of all, in the case of divorce, and she can take half of the patrimony of her partner and can keep her children with her. For women, it is the civil marriage, which will keep her safe. (Open text response: Civil marriage survey)

Likewise, this study finds that supporters of civil marriage believe the reform will advance women's rights in Lebanon, because civil marriage will enable women to gain an equal right to initiate divorce, retain a share of marital property, and retain child custody rights beyond the maternal custody period, stipulated in the respective personal status laws of Lebanon's fifteen personal status codes, as outlined in chapter 3. On the question of secularism, 84 percent of respondents agreed that there is a relationship between women's rights and the development of a secular framework for government and law in Lebanon. Importantly, the introduction of civil marriage and a unified civil status code is seen as a mechanism to unify the sects and harmonize women's rights across Lebanon's plural personal status codes. Moreover, civil marriage is viewed as the key to establishing a common national identity as Lebanese, as this participant advocates:

> [Civil marriage] would be the strongest, most peaceful, and most efficient way to change society's way of thinking, when people get used to the idea of secularism in mainstream society. And yes, civil marriage is a civil right that will slowly but surely break the power that religious leaders hold over people's decision making. It will affect values and shape views. It will affect the subconscious of society once these civil right values are taken in as the norm. How one defines him or herself will change. Identity will no longer be by sect, but by nationality. It is the first step to re-evaluate our identity as Lebanese. (Open text response: Online survey)

The argument for civil marriage reform, therefore, focuses on the role of interreligious civil unions in promoting two key societal changes. First, an equality of treatment between the genders across Lebanon's fifteen recognized personal status codes, including harmonizing women's rights between them, in relation to marriage and divorce, property rights, inheritance, and maternal custody rights,[11] as outlined in chapter 3. Second, civil marriage would promote the development of a unified national identity in

Lebanon, by shifting the jurisdiction of marriage from religious to civil law, thereby legalizing interreligious marriages and enabling couples from different sects to marry without converting, or listing their religion on their identity cards. With this legal change, religious endogamy will remain an option, but not a necessity, which can open the door for citizens to marry for "love and not religion."

In this study, overall, 25 percent of online survey respondents had contracted a civil marriage, 70 percent took place in Cyprus and 17 percent in Turkey, while three took place in Lebanon (13 percent). Of the civil marriages contracted overseas, overall, 42 percent had no family to attend the civil ceremony, while a minority also had a religious ceremony, 36 percent, and 56 percent of those marriages were also registered in a religious court. The civil marriages also registered in a religious court most will likely return to a Lebanese religious court, in the event of a divorce, for adjudication under the corresponding personal status code (Human Rights Watch 2015). The majority (64 percent) of respondents in this study described themselves as not being religious, while 21 percent said they were Christian and 15 percent Muslim, while the mean age of respondents was thirty-five years. To further understand the motivation of couples and their experiences of contracting a civil marriage, this study also undertook face-to-face interviews with ten civil marriage couples, as outlined in the methodology section in chapter 1. Three case study civil marriage stories are now presented.

CASE STUDY ONE

The first couple are both Muslim, one is Sunni and the other is Shi'ite; they chose to have a civil marriage in Lebanon in 2013. The wife explains why Lebanon needs a unified civil status code and what she sees as the advantage of civil marriage over religious marriage. She concludes with an explanation why she had a civil marriage and the significance of her decision for her child and for gender equality in Lebanon.

Q. What are the advantages or disadvantages of civil marriage?

For me, I see that the advantages are more than the disadvantages. Firstly, civil marriage is a door to communicate with the other sect. If we are going to talk of the sectarian regime, it opens the way among people to talk more about the other, to live together, and sometimes maybe to live in different regions in Lebanon. Civil marriage allows you to see Lebanon as all yours, not just a part of it and especially in our case when you want to go for civil marriage you have to drop your sect from the ID, this means you are not announcing that you are

Sunni or Shi'ite, or Maronite or whatever, for this reason this will open more doors for you to be a real citizen.

Q. Why did you have a civil marriage?

Because we both believe in our humanity and that life is a partnership. For me I do not want to be following the *sheikh's* authority, as I do not believe in them and I believe that they have corrupted the religion, so why should I give my life to someone who is not qualified enough to judge my life. Second, because there are some types of conflicts that might happen during your life where you want to be in control of everything and not any person, not any other *fatwas* or people that think they can be in your place. Also, when you have a civil marriage, as a woman, you are the one that says yes or no, while in the religious marriage, the Muslim one, you have to tell the *sheikh* that you are my representative and he goes and does it instead of me. From this point, you start not being responsible for yourself and I do not like this. I want to be free, I want to be in control of my life, I want to be a real partner to my husband and I want to share everything with him.

Q. Lastly, is civil marriage important for gender equality in Lebanon?

For me it is not the idea of gender, it is the idea of being human, but our problem is that our government and our people are not dealing with us as humans, not as free women and men. They are dealing with us as the sons and daughters of sects, as numbers to vote for them only. So, for this reason we need to know what is a human being, what are his/her rights/duties/responsibilities and then things will be fine between men and women, there won't be problems.

The core narrative in this interview is the desire to be in control of her own destiny, to take responsibility for her life back from clerical authority. Lastly, she sees the civil marriage project as integral to the process of becoming a free human being, not just being the "sons and daughters of sects." In order to achieve this, they chose a civil union and dropped their religion from their ID and from the ID of their newborn child.

CASE STUDY TWO

The second case study presents an interfaith couple, the wife is Sunni Muslim and the husband is Catholic. They chose to marry in Cyprus. The husband is more reticent, regarding their civil marriage, and consequently, only their close friends know that they opted for the "Cyprus solution." The problematic issue of conversion between religions, as Muslim women are not permitted in Islamic family law to marry non-Muslims, and the rights of women in divorce were the key factors in their decision to go ahead with a civil marriage, rather than a religious marriage:

Q. Why did you have a civil marriage?

Because my husband and I are from different religions and my parents did not accept that I follow my husband's religion, so we decided to go midway and have a civil marriage. By the way my husband does not admit that he got a civil marriage, he tells everyone he went for a Christian one in Cyprus. Only our close friends that joined us in Cyprus know this fact.

Q. Should a civil status code be introduced in Lebanon?

The current one is not fair for women, because if the man wants a divorce he can have it without consenting with his wife and he can just deprive her of her rights. And that is why I have gone for a civil marriage, I cannot be living under the mercy of a *sheikh* or a cleric. Mainly the custody of children is important, as it still applies old laws. For example, the girl's custody age is different than boys. When they are most in need of their mums at puberty, this is when they can be taken away. We took a religious marriage ceremony, as a first step, which was not lodged in the religious court, so that my parents would accept the civil marriage, as Muslim women we are not supposed to convert to our husband's religion.

The custody of children and the rights of women in divorce were significant factors behind the decision for this woman to decide in favor of civil marriage. The civil union was presented as a halfway point, which enabled neither party to contravene the rules of their religion. The difficulty of conversion for Muslim women, wishing to marry across religious lines, was also raised as an important factor in favor of civil marriage, as it enabled her parents to agree to the union. The couple also lodged the marriage contract in a religious court, so that her parents would consent to the marriage. But in the case of divorce, the corresponding personal status code will likely take precedence over the civil marriage.

CASE STUDY THREE

The third couple are both Catholics and the key issue for them was the right to divorce, which is particularly difficult for Maronite Catholics in Lebanon. The wife explains that her husband's prior divorce, and the difficulties he encountered in concluding his divorce, was a key factor in their decision-making. She also notes that in Islam divorces are difficult, as women risk losing custody of their children and face financial difficulties. Consequently, when they weighed up the options, they decided to go to Turkey for a civil marriage to guarantee the future outcome if the marriage fails:

> Most people look at civil marriage as a contract. Religious marriages are so costly, especially in Christianity. Most people believe that civil marriage will give both parties their rights, in the case of divorce, whereas in religious marriages, there is always one party that suffers more than the other. I must add that in Christianity divorce is a nightmare. It is almost impossible to get a divorce without changing religion, paying a fortune, or having to wait for years and years. The process of divorce is very difficult also in Islam. Very few women get the right to care for their children and have enough money to look after them themselves. It is very ironic to talk about the divorce and advantages of divorce in a civil marriage, rather than talk about the marriage itself. However, since we have witnessed so many divorces gone bad, people can't but think of the end rather than the means. I want a clean and civilized separation or divorce. So, civil marriage it was. (Online Interview, Beirut October 2013)

The difficulties of obtaining a divorce led this couple to decide in advance to make their lives easier if the marriage didn't work out. Most importantly, in this case study, the interviewee wants to make sure that she has the right to custody of her children, if the marriage should end in divorce. The wife notes that she doesn't like to be pessimistic and think of the separation before the marriage, but considering the difficulties her husband has had, she decided to ensure a clean and civilized separation. She notes that Catholicism makes the recognition of divorce almost impossible, given the rules of annulment, as outlined in chapter 3, such that it is very costly and usually does not work out, leading Christian men to either opt for conversion to Islam, in order to remarry, or opt for a civil marriage overseas. The advantage of a civil marriage, as outlined in this case, is that all the problems of marriage and divorce are worked out in advance and the rights of each partner are guaranteed, based on civil law, not religious law.

THE ARGUMENT AGAINST CIVIL MARRIAGE REFORM

However, not everyone is convinced that civil marriage will resolve Lebanon's women's rights deficit and confessional woes. Rather, there are some distinct disadvantages and limitations, which are noted in the argument against civil marriage. Moreover, the opposition to civil marriage reform is more pronounced among Muslims than Christians. While civil marriage could offer an innovative solution to the confessional contradictions in Lebanon, it also represents a radical departure from long-standing cultural and marriage practices, based upon endogamous marriage within the kin group and homogamous marriage within the sect, as outlined in chapter 3, which are supported by the structure of Lebanon's plural personal status codes, in which interreligious marriages are difficult, require conversion, or are not recognized. Moreover, the status quo underpins the relative power balance between the sects, within Lebanon's confessional political system. Hence, opposition to civil marriage rests on the view that moving the jurisdiction of marriage from religious to civil law will, first, weaken the power of religious courts to determine matters of a marriage, divorce, and the custody of children and, second, weaken the autonomy of each confession. Consequently, the obstacles to its broader adoption are significant.

In order to understand the opposition to civil marriage, in greater depth, participants in this study were asked why there is opposition to the introduction of civil marriages in Lebanon. One respondent offered the view that "Lebanon is a conglomeration of sectarian entities . . . threatened by any law that treats the Lebanese as a single homogeneous society, rather than a mosaic of warring factions." A word cloud of responses from 108 open text responses to the question, why is there opposition to civil marriage, in the online survey on civil marriage (2013) (see figure 6.3), found the top five key words used to explain the opposition to civil marriage in Lebanon were, in the following order of significance: religion (40 percent of responses), people

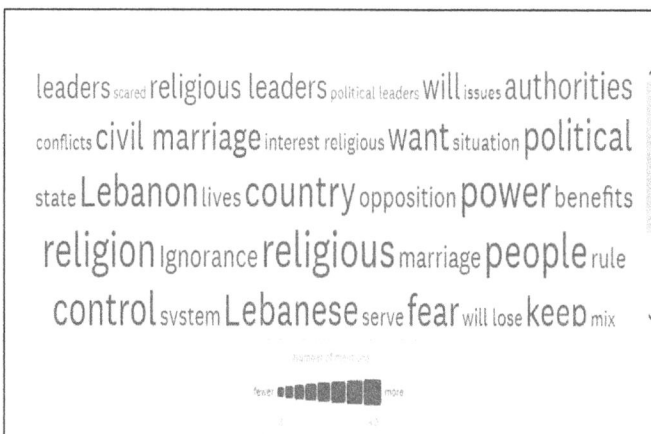

Figure 6.3 Word Cloud of Key Words Depicting the Opposition to Civil Marriage Reform. *Source*: Online civil marriage survey 2013.

(16 percent), power (15 percent), and control (9 percent). Moreover, one respondent characterizes Lebanon as a "religious dictatorship" and argues that religious authorities

> control personal lives and make barricades between communities of the same nation . . . and impose codes concerning marriage and the inequality of women and men. (Open text response: Civil marriage survey 2013)

Despite a clear view that religious authorities oppose civil marriage reform, there appears to be a large attitudinal gap between the new wave of feminist activists and civil marriage advocates, who comprised 54 percent of respondents to the online civil marriage survey and broader popular opinion in Lebanon on this issue. By contrast, a large offline social survey of 2,000 respondents on civil marriage attitudes, undertaken by The Status of Women in the Middle East and North Africa (SWMENA 2011, 2), found that 54 percent of men and 64 percent of women are opposed to its broader adoption, as well as the leading religious clerics in Lebanon. Moreover, the practice of civil marriage is particularly opposed by Sunnis (74 percent of men and 81 percent of women), and Shi'ites (68 percent of men and 78 percent of women), while Catholics are more in favor of it, with 63 percent of men and 55 percent of women in favor. The higher acceptance rate of civil marriage among Catholics in Lebanon, it is surmised, is attributable to their greater difficulty in obtaining access to divorce, under the Catholic personal status code; a finding supported by face-to-face interviews conducted in this study with civil marriage couples, outlined earlier in this chapter.

In considering the reasons for Muslim opposition to civil marriage, El-Cheikh (1998, 156) concluded that Shi'ite religious clerics "tried to reconcile the secular and clerical positions and, nevertheless, found the option of civil marriage to be superfluous." In Islamic *Shari'a* law, she argued, marriage is already practiced as a contract, rather than a sacrament, as is the case under Catholic Ecclesiastical law (Nichols 2012b, 11–60). Hence, for clerics, a civil marriage contract offered no additional innovation, over what is already available within the Muslim personal status codes. Additionally, Muslim women are not permitted to marry non-Muslims, under Islamic family law, and in the event of an interfaith marriage, the husband should convert to the wife's religion for the marriage to proceed. However, Muslim men can marry Christian or Jewish women under the Islamic family law. Additionally, some Christian churches, notably the Orthodox churches, will not marry a Christian and Muslim (IECCEC 2000). Conversion between religions remains the largest sticking point for interfaith couples. Nevertheless, among Muslims, the Shi'ites are more open to civil marriage than the Sunni or Druze sects, according to this interviewee:

> The Shi'ites are more open than the Sunni to civil marriage. I never met a Sunni accepting of civil marriage. [For the] Druze it is out of the question, they won't accept it. I think Maronites and Christians are more open to this marriage, though it took me some time to convince my husband of it. It is his dream to have a marriage at the Church and civil, as his mom dreamt of us at the church getting married and wanted this to happen. My community and my religion do not allow me to do this. I am a believer, but not a fanatic. (Interview, Beirut 2015)

Supporters of civil marriage argue that the advantage of civil marriage is that neither party has to convert for an interreligious marriage to be contracted. Opponents of civil marriage, by contrast, argue that Islam introduced many rights not currently recognized by the Christian personal status codes, including the marital contract, *niqa*, the bride price, *maher*, which women retain if the husband initiates unilateral divorce, the right to maintenance and support, while married, and the right for women to initiate divorce, under certain conditions (Moghadam 2004), as outlined in chapter 3. The only limitation is in the implementation of women's rights, within the provisions of the Muslim personal status codes, as this interviewee highlights:

> Traditional marriage is not a fair marriage for women, especially for Muslims. The *Qur'an* says that the woman has a lot of rights, unfortunately the implementation is not as what is written. If my husband wants to divorce me, he can do it, without my opinion and I will find myself with nothing. He can have a second and third wife and I can't complain. . . . Civil marriage gives us equal rights with the same religion or with mixed religious marriages, my husband is a Maronite and I admire him a lot, he respects my religion, sect, family and everything more than any man I would ever meet . . . civil marriage is here to make our lives easier. (Interview, Beirut 2015)

While contrasting viewpoints on civil marriage are evident and the acceptance of a secular alternative varies between religious sects, on current indications, the acceptance of civil marriage in Lebanon is some way off. While this study has found a high rate of acceptance of civil marriage among young people and activists from a variety of religious backgrounds, this contrasts with a broader public and clerical opinion in Lebanon, as noted above (SWMENA 2011, 2). Moreover, to date, a civil marriage law has not been passed by the parliament, despite the first civil marriage contracted on Lebanese soil in 2013. As such, the reform of personal status codes and the introduction of civil marriage remain unresolved.

DISCUSSION

Having reviewed the argument for and against civil marriage, and the views of civil marriage couples themselves, there is no clear consensus in this debate. While civil marriage might make life easier for interfaith marriages, the reluctance to marry "across sectarian lines" is, nonetheless, a common finding across the region, especially in societies marked by high degrees of conflict and strong religious divides. In neighboring Israel, there is low tolerance, overall, for interfaith relationships in a conflict zone. Rather, a study found an entrenched preference for endogamous marriage and homogamy, in order to maintain cultural identity and the status quo (Siham Yahya 2016). In counterpoint, advocates of civil marriage in Lebanon argue that without reforming the system of plural, religious family law and introducing a unified civil status code for civil marriage, Lebanon's confessional contradictions will continue in a vicious cycle, and homogamy and endogamy will remain the only legal option available.

Civil marriage may, indeed, offer an innovative solution to the women's rights puzzle in Lebanon; it also represents a radical departure from longstanding marriage practices, based upon endogamous marriage within the sect and, indeed, the kin group, which underpins Lebanon's confessional system, as outlined in chapter 3. Moreover, civil marriage will weaken the power of religious courts to determine matters of a marriage, divorce, and the custody of children; so consequently, the obstacles to its broader adoption are significant, as one interviewee philosophically warns:

> When both sexes have equal rights, and have equal responsibilities in marriage life and in divorce, then both sexes will feel the urgency to work together. The male ego in a male governed society is unbreakable. . . . Male chauvinist societies cannot and will not accept that women can be their equal. It is simple and it is clear. As long as priests and *sheikhs* are being bribed . . . as long as politicians' only objective is their own pocket . . . well . . . there is not much hope. (Online Interview, Beirut October 2013)

Time will tell how this process of social transformation plays out, but the winds of change are in the air, as couples seek solutions, which work around Lebanon's plural personal status codes, by either going overseas to Cyprus or taking their chances with the old French Mandate law, 60LR.

CONCLUSION

The civil marriage debate highlights the unique character of negotiations over women's rights and citizen's rights in the case of Lebanon. While civil marriage potentially offers an innovative solution to the women's rights puzzle in Lebanon, the barriers to its broader adoption are many. The analysis found that the movement for civil marriage reform integrates an intersectional understanding of the nature of women's inequality in Lebanon as deriving from both patriarchal social norms and the sectarian social and political structure of the Lebanese polity. In this regard, women's rights and civil rights are mutually reinforcing. Lebanon's system of legal pluralism leads women to experience differential rights to divorce and child custody. Advocates emphasize two key social reforms to improve civil rights and women's rights: (1) the introduction of a unified civil status code to harmonize the system of plural, religious family law across all codes and to ensure a minimum age of marriage, and (2) equal access to divorce, child custody, and marital property. As the interviews with civil marriage couples highlight, the introduction of an optional civil marriage law would facilitate interreligious and secular marriage without the need for conversion between religions. Advocates argued that these reforms would move the jurisdiction of marriage from religious to civil law and resolve the contradiction between citizenship and religious affiliation, improving both civil rights and women's rights. Opponents of civil marriage view the reform as a social revolution that would progressively dismantle Lebanon's confessional system through a secularization process, which limits the autonomy of the personal status code system. Most importantly, for opponents the introduction of civil marriage has the potential to transform the mode of self-identification in Lebanon from sect to nation, by legalizing interreligious marriage, which is currently opposed by the major religions in Lebanon. This debate cannot be resolved in the short term, due to political, clerical, and social barriers to the adoption of civil marriage, despite rising public support for the change, as noted by the interviewees and survey respondents in this chapter. In the long term, however, the recognition of Lebanon's first civil marriage in 2013 under 60LR opens the door to novel solutions that bypass both Lebanon's personal status and legislative systems, to bring about social change from the ground up.

NOTES

1. Civil marriage is defined as "The formal union of a man and a woman, typically recognized by law, by which they become husband and wife, a similar long-term relationship between partners of the same sex." *The New Oxford American Dictionary* (Kindle Locations 501680-501683) (Oxford University Press. Kindle Edition, 2005).

2. In the case of Lebanon's civil marriage debate, the recognition of same-sex civil unions is not the primary focus of the movement, but rather, heterosexual couples seeking a civil union outside of the system of plural religious family law.

However, it is advocated that the rights of same-sex couples would also be significantly improved if such a law was introduced in Lebanon.

3. Israeli couples who also go there for civil unions, as there is no civil marriage law in Israel.

4. See the facts and figures compiled here, while not definitive, they are only indicative: http://ginosblog.com/2013/01/19/facts-and-figures-on-civil-marriage-in -lebanon/.

5. Ibid.

6. See Nadia Travel, http://www.nadiatravel.com/?page_id=661&category=51.

7. Article 25 of 60LR recognizes foreign civil marriage laws for the purpose of divorce in Lebanon.

8. See the following article by Martin Chulov (2019). *Guardian Newspaper*, https://www.theguardian.com/world/2019/aug/25/lebandon-high-society-wedding -tests-civil-freedom.

9. See Knutsen and Hassanl, *The Daily Star,* http://www.dailystar.com.lb/ News/Lebanon-News/2015/Mar-02/289250-hundreds-march-for-civil-marriagsec ularism.ashx?utm_source=Magnet&utm_medium=Related%20Articles%20widget& utm_campaign=Magnet%20tools.

10. Of respondents to the civil marriage survey 83 percent live in Lebanon and 48.2 percent were female and 51.8 percent were male, while 64 percent identified as being not religious, 20.6 percent as Christian, and 15.4 percent as being Muslim.

11. There currently is a limited period of maternal custody, which varies by the child's age for each personal status code; see chapter 3 for details.

Chapter 7

Conclusion

Caught between Sect and Nation

INTRODUCTION

This study asked, *is secular citizenship the key to resolving the women's rights puzzle in Lebanon?* To answer the research question, part I of the book, *Formations*, examined the formation of Lebanon as a confessional democracy and explored the plural system of personal status law in Lebanon, wherein women experience differential and relational rights under both religious and civil law. Part II of the book, *Activism*, then examined the development of the Lebanese women's movement and online/offline campaigns for the introduction of a domestic violence law in 2014, in chapter 4, and intersectional campaigns for women's nationality rights, the adoption of a women's quota in parliament, and to resolve the garbage crisis in 2015, in chapter 5. The quest for civil marriage reform was examined in chapter 6, by considering the arguments for the reform presented by case study civil marriage couples and the argument against the reform, based on interviews and online survey results. The book found that, under the eighteen recognized personal status codes, married women become "wards" of their husbands upon marriage, with guardianship passing from their father to their husband, while civil rights are relational and follow a patrilineal logic. Concomitant to the dual legal system, which makes a division between the jurisdiction of religious and civil laws, there is an associated tension between the status of all Lebanese as subjects of their sect, *ahlin*, in a kin-based collectivity under a corresponding personal status code, and their individual rights to equality as citizens, *muwatinin*, of the nation-state. Women are caught between sect and nation and, consequently, experience separate and unequal rights under both religious and civil law.

The possibility to expand women's rights by reforming personal status law to strengthen the conjugal family over the patrilineage, as Charrad (2001) demonstrated in her study of the *Maghribi* states, will be determined by similar state formation processes, in the case of Lebanon. Ultimately the power of kin-based groups was limited in favor of a centralized state formation, in the case of Tunisia. Lebanon is in the midst of a similar transition. Given the recognition of eighteen religious communities, which compete with the nation-state, as a mode of identification, and which limit women's rights within the family, shifting the balance from religious to civil laws, and in so doing, shifting the mode of identification from sect to nation, will be a necessary, but not sufficient process, to consolidate women's rights in Lebanon. Hence, a social revolution is underway in Lebanon, as documented by the campaigns, which were examined in this book.

Moreover, until citizenship laws are revised, women's citizenship rights and sectarian affiliation will remain relational, first, passed through their father and, second, through their husband, in accordance with the rules of patrilineal descent. Hence, nationality rights are lost upon marriage to a foreign husband. The irony is that women reproduce both sect and nation, yet they do not fully belong to either. As has been shown in this book, the Lebanese consociational system, which is unique in the Middle East, manages two key forms of difference, the first based upon religious affiliation and the second, based upon gender. It guarantees the absolute freedom of faith but allocates relational rights to women, based upon their religious affiliation and marital status, as a married woman's citizenship status is contingent upon her husband. Thus, in a hierarchy of rights, religious autonomy and consociational representation in government receives greater provision than gender equality. Thus, a secular transition is necessary to resolve the women's rights puzzle in Lebanon, as citizenship status will become absolute, irrespective of sect or gender, rather than relational based upon sect and gender.

However, as was shown in chapters 3 to 6, patriarchy is also a social and political construct in which male domination and the guardianship of women transcend both religious and secular law, hence, the transformation of civil and criminal laws is also necessary to improve gender equality in Lebanon. The key dilemma the Lebanese consociational system faces, going forward, is the trade-off between competing rights: first, to religious difference, second, to equal citizenship rights, irrespective of gender. Currently the system is skewed in favor of perpetuating religious difference, as a form of self and group identification, at the expense of identification with the nation. Gender equality remains the missing link, leaving women's status caught between sect and nation.

THE WOMEN'S RIGHTS PUZZLE IN
LEBANON: LESSONS LEARNED

In considering the lessons learned, in the course of this book, regarding the nature of the women's rights puzzle in Lebanon, the first part of the book, *Formations*, started with chapter 2, which examined the formation of Lebanon as a confessional democracy and the origins of women's second-class status within Lebanon's system of family law, which is based upon autonomous personal status codes for the eighteen recognized religious communities in Lebanon. This chapter discussed the history of Lebanon and the evolution of Lebanon's consociational power-sharing system, which divides political power between eighteen recognized religious sects. The chapter started with a discussion of the pre-Ottoman and Ottoman history, the French Mandate, Independence, the civil war, and the Second Republic. The chapter concluded with a discussion of the implications of Lebanon's confessional system for gender relations and the challenges of reproducing sect and nation, women's relational citizenship rights and the precarious state of postcolonial Lebanon.

Chapter 3 examined Lebanon's system of legal pluralism and the evolution of the division between civil and religious law, dating back to the French Mandate. While the Ottomans developed the *millet* system, whereby subjects of non-Muslim religious affiliations were governed in accordance with their faith, this mode of governing religious difference was codified into fifteen separate personal status codes for eighteen recognized religious confessions in Lebanon during the French Mandate. This chapter examined how the personal status codes were developed and the system of family law, which operates in Lebanon today. The chapter started by discussing the anthropology of marriage systems and the trend toward the democratization of personal relationships and marriage. The chapter then examined the differences between the Christian and Muslim personal status codes in relation to marriage, divorce, marital property, alimony, and child custody rights. The chapter concluded with a discussion of the discrimination against women within civil or secular laws. The chapter found that women experience separate and unequal rights across all of Lebanon's personal status codes and under all codes they become wards (*female coverture*) of their husband upon marriage.

Part II of the book, *Activism*, started with chapter 4, which examined the new phase of women's rights activism in Lebanon and the emergence of several online/offline campaigns for social change. The development of the Lebanese women's movement across four phases of activism was considered. The chapter then examined the role of digital activism, as part of the new tool kit that contemporary women's rights activists deploy in the Arab Spring, and the role of new media strategies of communication, which utilize online/

offline modes of activism to engage citizens in critical issues, bypassing old media channels and established political processes. The chapter concluded that the iterative movement between online and offline modes of activism had enabled social change to progress during a political deadlock. The case of Lebanon's domestic violence law of 2014 was examined, which demonstrated that compromise was necessary to achieve law reform, given that the marital rape provision was not, ultimately, removed from the legislation.

Chapter 5 examined the intersection between women's rights campaigns in Lebanon and broader social and political movements that have emerged in the last five years. The campaigns overlap and address a broad array of social and political grievances that Lebanese have experienced with the state, or its absence. From women's nationality rights, to electoral reform and the #YouStink garbage campaigns, at the height of Lebanon's garbage crisis in 2015, the campaigns showed the intersection between the women's rights deficit and the deadlock in Lebanon's political system. The chapter examined the links between these seemingly disparate campaigns and the extended deadlock in Lebanon's government and the political and social campaigns to improve women's citizenship rights, expand their representation in parliament, address the problem of sectarianism, and tackle the ecological crisis arising from poor public administration. The key lesson learned in this chapter was the intersectional character of the women's rights debate in Lebanon. Without the reform of nationality rights, women will not have full citizenship rights, irrespective of their marital status. Second, without a women's quota, improving their representation in parliament is stubbornly slow and Lebanon's parliament will continue to have one of the lowest proportions of women in the world, because the sectarian quota trumps the women's quota. Ironically, without improving the representation of women in parliament, it is difficult to pass progressive legislation, which would resolve the other three key women's rights campaigns examined in this book: domestic violence, women's nationality rights, and civil marriage law reform. Finally, the Lebanese system remains precarious due to the complexity of forming government under the consociational system, leading to frequent deadlocks and political impasses, which leaves public administration and governance neglected, as was the case in 2015, leading to the garbage crisis. Hence, Lebanese feminism is intersectional, because the sectarian question and the women's rights question are interconnected.

Finally, chapter 6 considered the movement for civil marriage reform, perhaps the most contentious women's rights issue in Lebanon. The debate raises important questions regarding women's location between sect and nation in Lebanon due to the absence of a civil marriage law and unified civil status code for matters relating to marriage, divorce, inheritance, and child custody. While not the first time a civil marriage law has been introduced in

Lebanon, the recognition of Lebanon's first civil marriage in 2013 reignited the national debate. This chapter started by examining the argument for civil marriage, and then considered three case study civil marriage couples to understand their reasons for seeking a civil marriage, then the argument against the recognition of civil marriage was presented. The chapter found that the civil marriage debate will not be resolved in the short term, despite growing acceptance among advocates and youth, as highlighted by the interviews and online survey results, because of clerical opposition to the reform and broader societal attitudes, which are still largely opposed to the adoption of civil marriage in Lebanon, particularly among Muslims. Nonetheless, couples have found loopholes in the personal status code system, and either gone abroad to contract a civil marriage in Cyprus or contracted a civil marriage at home in Lebanon, by taking their chances with the old French Mandate civil law, 60LR. Hence, a quiet social revolution is taking place, which bypasses official laws and political processes, to shift marriage from the jurisdiction of religious law to civil law, enabling interfaith and secular marriages.

DEBATES ON PERSONAL STATUS LAW, SECULARISM, AND RELIGIOUS DIFFERENCE

Given the nature of the women's rights puzzle in Lebanon, whereby women are caught between sect and nation, this book examined whether the concept of secular citizenship can resolve the contradiction. It was found that secularism, the separation of religion and politics, is largely a Western construct, which derives from Enlightenment Europe but cannot so easily be mapped onto a Middle Eastern context, because it assumes that class is the main form of social division. However, Charrad (2001) and Joseph (1996) have argued, to the contrary, that kin-based groupings and their intersection with state formation processes are one of the major differences between the Middle East, including Lebanon, and the development of "citizenship" and the "nation-state" in Europe and the West. While the secularization thesis holds that modernization is coupled with secularization, there are two exceptions to the international trend, the Middle Eastern region and the United States of America (Dobbelaere 1999). Rather, in the Middle Eastern region experiments in secular governance have largely failed, such as the Baathist regimes of Iraq and Syria and Nasserist Egypt. Second, a resurgent Islamist current can be found across the region, with some gaining power through the ballot box, as is the case in Turkey, or for a short period in post-Arab Spring Egypt, or shared power, as was the case in Tunisia (Noueihed and Warren 2012). Meanwhile, Israel announced a Jewish citizenship law in 2018[1] and the Islamic State of the Levant and Syria (ISIS/ISIL) declared an Islamic caliphate, which was largely defeated in 2018. The key challenge in a region of diverse religions, kin-based groupings, and pluralist societies is how secular governance can recognize religious difference, while safeguarding that majority religions do not rule over minority religions, or vice versa.

Lebanon is such an experiment. Since its independence from the French Mandate in 1943, the Lebanese system of governance has been based upon a hybrid system, referred to as a confessional democracy, as outlined in chapter 2. Confessional democracy is a consociational power-sharing system, designed to ensure the equitable representation of all recognized religious sects within the system of government. However, the relative distribution of roles, seats, and portfolios in parliament have been significantly disputed since Lebanon gained independence, in particular the allocation of the presidency to the Maronites, and the proportion of Christians to Muslims in parliament, overall, with the Christians receiving the majority of seats in parliament under the National Pact, following a ratio of 6:5 (Traboulsi 2012), as outlined in chapter 2. The system of confessional democracy survived the civil war, between 1975 and 1990, and following the Ta'if accord, which ended the war, a Second Republic was founded in 1990 (Hage 2001). However, in the new republic the role of the presidency was downgraded and balanced with that of the prime minister, although the allocation of roles within the executive was still based on sect. Meanwhile, the distribution of seats in the legislative branch was still based on sect but was balanced between Christian and Muslim sects overall on the basis of parity 5:5, and 128 overall (Traboulsi 2012). However, two key contradictions persist in the consociational system overall. First, the dual conception of Lebanese as both citizens, *muwatinin,* of the nation and subjects of their religious community, *ahlin.* Second, Lebanese women find themselves caught between sect and nation, in the crosshairs of the dual legal system, which underpins the hybrid political system. Lebanon is a hybrid, when comparing multi-communal states. According to Hanf (1993), with a syncretistic national ideology, which recognizes cultural differences, coexistence has been achieved following armed conflict. The challenge multi-communal states face is "how to regulate conflicts between peoples, ethnic groups, religious and linguistic communities coexisting within one state" (Hanf 1993, 9). Lebanon's approach, to this central problem, has been to make a division between civil and religious law and grant autonomy to each religious community, to govern their own matters of personal status. In so doing, religious autonomy is privileged over national unity and women's equality is the casualty of the National Pact.

The transition from subject to citizen was a key process in the formation of nation-states, following the enlightenment ideas of the French Revolution (Sherman, Gould, and Ansari 2014). Likewise, the transition in marriage "in progressive societies," as noted by Sir Henry Maine, was from marriages based on personal status to contract (Wright 1984; Garrison 1983), a transition also noted by feminist legal theory (Pateman 1988). However, in the Middle Eastern states, no such linear transition from subject to citizen, or in marriage, from status to contract can be traced. Moreover, Pateman (1988) theorizes that it does not necessarily follow that women's equality is guaranteed by a contract, which can still encode their subordination. Second, within Islamic family law, marriage was never practiced as an enduring personal status or sacrament; it has always been a contract. Thus, in the case of Lebanon, a secularization, or "modernization" process, will not necessarily resolve all the contradictions of the consociational system, wherein Lebanese are both citizens and subjects, as noted earlier. Likewise, for women, both status and contract marriages already exist; the issue is whether marriage will be a contract between equals. Moreover, the persistence of women's economic and political inequality, won't be resolved through transforming the marriage contract alone. Although these two propositions have been central to the women's rights and civil rights campaigns examined in this book, in chapters 4, 5, and 6, and the views expressed in interviews with civil marriage couples, this book finds that applying a Western, secular solution (citizens and contracts), as such, will not completely resolve the women's rights puzzle in Lebanon. Rather, a cosmopolitan framework for citizenship and an optional civil marriage law would be a step in the right direction, because it would allow for the recognition of religious difference, while making the application of plural personal status law for marriage an option, alongside a secular alternative. A cosmopolitan approach is an approach to balance thick and thin values, reflecting women's rights within diverse contexts. The key challenge is "to develop a conception of citizenship that accommodates plural, particularistic and often antagonistic identities without tearing apart the society" (Fisher Onar and Paker 2012, 2). Reconciling thin commitments, which are universal, such as women's rights, with thick, divergent practices, as is the case with Lebanon's dual legal system and pluralistic society, is an enduring challenge, but an optional, unified civil status code is a step in the right direction.

TOWARD A UNIFIED CIVIL STATUS CODE?

In the face of opposition to such a change, it does not seem likely that a unified code will be introduced any time soon in Lebanon. While the president supported the recognition of a unified civil status code and the Ministry of the Interior recognized the first civil marriage contracted on Lebanese soil on April 25, 2013 (Aziz 2013), religious opposition has remained, particularly among Muslim religious leaders. The recognition of Lebanon's first civil marriage in 2013 set the precedent for further change on this issue. However, Lebanon's first civil marriage couple ultimately moved to Sweden, due to the scale of the media publicity their case attracted, the continued opposition of religious leaders, and the government's decision, ultimately, not to recognize any further civil marriages.[2]

Those in support of a secular framework, an *'almani* system, for family law, argue it will "return religious institutions to the business of religion and not politics" (Zalzal 1997). It is argued that civil laws guarantee human rights, and equality, while religion will become a private affiliation but not a legal status. Nonetheless, the French 60LR law remains on the books in Lebanon, but its implementation is difficult, as noted in chapter 6. The legal loophole, which enabled its implementation, was that couples struck their religious affiliation from their ID, which means they were "excommunicated" from their religion, in order to marry under the civil law. Meanwhile, all other attempts to introduce a unified civil status code for family affairs have not been passed by parliament, despite repeated attempts since 1973, as noted in chapter 5. Myriam Sfier, a deputy head of the Lebanese Institute for women's studies (now Arab Institute for Women), at the Lebanese American University, noted, in a published speech, that "we need a unified civil code to protect women's rights, we shouldn't all follow the husband, we should be civil citizens, civil people."[3] While the government moves from crisis to crisis, the law remains unchanged, despite the Ta'if accord, which settled the civil war containing a clause that Lebanon should eventually move from a "confessional to a secular" system of governance (Traboulsi 2012). Meanwhile, in the absence of legislative or political change, couples continue to work around existing personal status laws, by contracting civil marriages overseas, or trying their luck with LR60, from the French Mandate. The unified personal status code and civil marriage debate will continue until a new balance between religious and secular law can be found, in which the latter takes precedence.

FUTURE PROSPECTS

Italy was the last state in Europe to approve a civil union law, which recognized same-sex couples on February 25, 2016,[4] despite opposition from the Roman Catholic Church, while Turkey and Tunisia were the first states in the MENA region to adopt a civil marriage law, as noted in chapter 3. Europe now allows both civil marriage and same-sex civil unions in most jurisdictions, while MENA only allows civil marriage in two states, and same-sex unions are not recognized in any jurisdictions.[5] The secularization of family law remains a key impediment across the region and Lebanon faces particular challenges, as outlined by the debates put forward by advocates and couples in this book. The dual legal system remains the key impediment, which makes a division between the jurisdiction of religious and secular law, the former pertaining to the family, the latter to civil and criminal law. The division between the two, a fusion between the Ottoman and French legal systems (Thompson 2000), guarantees the jurisdiction of religious law over family law, which limits interreligious marriages between sects and maintains endogamy within the eighteen recognized religious sects in Lebanon (Zalzal 1997).[6]

Conversion between religions is highly gendered within Lebanon. As discussed in chapter 6, Muslim women are not permitted to marry non-Muslims and convert, rather the inverse direction of conversion must apply, the opposite is true of Christian women, as Muslim men are permitted to marry Christian or Jewish women (Zalzal 1997). Yet, there are Christian confessions, notably Orthodox and Catholic that do not permit marriage between Christians and non-Christians. What is more, much is lost in the process of conversion, most importantly inheritance rights for Muslim women, as Islamic law does not permit Christians to inherit. Since 1959, Christian sects inherit based on a civil law, while Muslim sects inherit based on the *Shari'a*. In all confessions, women lose maternal custody rights upon conversion, due to the obligation to educate children in the father's religious confession. While it is true that legal dualism grants a high degree of autonomy to the religious confessions to administer their own personal status laws, in accordance with the relevant code of their confession, the system also divides citizens into subjects of their confession, in order to reproduce the confessional political system as a whole. Moreover, the secularization of family law remains a contested issue between state and religious authority, raising the question, which should take precedence? As the chapters of this book have shown, the latter prevails, at the expense of women's right to egalitarian treatment before the law, irrespective of their sectarian affiliation.

Of course, the irony of the consociational system is that it is designed to ensure the proportional representation of each sect in government, due to a quota system, which no longer reflects the relative distribution of each sect's share of the population. Hence, there has not been a formal census in Lebanon since 1932, as discussed in the preface and chapter 2, but it is expected that such a census would show that Christians, while once constituting a demographic majority, are now 37 percent of the population (Economist 2016), owing to a higher share of migration over the course of a century but especially during the civil war. The sectarian distribution of seats and cabinet posts necessitates a constant consideration of the relative "confessional mix," the numerical distribution of each sect, and their overall power allocation in the numbers game between the sects. Indeed, Farha (2012, 380) argues, the consociational answer to societal pluralism "poses a new set of challenges, the most daunting of which is the periodic recalibration of the political representations of regions, parties and sects, so as to reflect inescapable demographic vacillations." Moreover, while Switzerland in 2003 readjusted their "magic formula," Lebanon regularly descends into dangerous political deadlocks (Farha 2012, 380).

Overall, while sectarian quotas were meant to ensure an equitable representation between sects, the implementation of the Lebanese system, in practice, has guaranteed the opposite, with dispute and contestation prevailing. Not only does consociational accommodation result in periodic episodes of malaise and protracted deadlocks, the maintenance of the "mix" justifies illiberalism in all matters of personal status, for overtly political outcomes. The lack of recognition of Palestinian citizens' rights, who remain stateless in Lebanon, and women's nationality rights are both examples of paradoxes, noted in this book, which preserve the "balance" between Christians and Muslims, as outlined in chapters 5 and 6. Moreover, the cost of sectarian accommodation has been the development of a unified national identity and gender equality (Farha 2012, 376).

One is left with the conclusion that a more egalitarian political arrangement would not distribute seats in government and cabinet posts on the basis of sectarian quotas but rather on the basis of a democratic election process, based on non-sectarian political parties and policy accountability. This would guarantee personal religious freedoms but "separate religion and politics" in matters of law and political process. Thus, as the social movements and women's rights campaigns examined in this book have shown, there is a gap between the theory and practice of consociationalism, which leaves women's rights caught between two key competing political commitments. First, to communal religious difference and second, to equality as Lebanese citizens, based on universal principles enshrined by the United Nations and in the Lebanese constitution, irrespective of sect or gender. Balancing these two competing imperatives will be the challenge for Lebanon, going forward, as a new generation of globalized, educated, Lebanese youth seek civil rights and gender equality, a challenge which the system of confessional democracy has yet to meet. Hence, there are two parallel social movements, which continue in Lebanon—the first for political rights and the second for personal status law reform to ensure gender equality between citizens, not subjects. The events of October 2019 demonstrate the ongoing nature of Lebanon's transformation.

CONCLUSION

This study asked, *is secular citizenship the key to resolving the women's rights puzzle in Lebanon?* To answer the research question, the book explored the plural system of personal status law in Lebanon and showed that women experience differential rights, under both religious and civil law. It found that the consociational division of power between sect and nation in Lebanon results in a gender equality deficit. A secular transition is necessary but not sufficient to resolve the women's rights puzzle in Lebanon, as women's nationality rights are forfeited upon marriage to a foreign husband and cannot be transmitted to their children. However, through a recalibration of religious and secular laws, so that the latter prevail over the former, citizenship status will no longer be relational based on sect or gender. Moreover, an optional unified civil status code will transform religious marriage into an option but not a necessity, as is the case in other jurisdictions globally, where civil marriage laws have been implemented. However, as was shown in chapters 5 and 6, patriarchal modes of societal organization, enshrined in patrilineal religious codes, and economic and political systems with low rates of female participation perpetuate male domination and the guardianship of women as "wards of their husband" in a vicious cycle. As such, the transformation of civil and criminal laws is not sufficient to improve gender equality in Lebanon, without a revision of the relative relationship between religion and politics in Lebanon. A rebalancing of the power between the two sides of Lebanon's dual legal system is necessary, so that civil law, ultimately, prevails over religious law, rather than simply reenforcing the imperatives of patriarchal religious law in matters of personal status. Thus, it is concluded that the key dilemma for the Lebanese consociational system, going forward, is to revisit the "magic balance" between sect and nation, to ensure gender equality. In so doing, many other societal and political transformations will follow, as the relationship between the marriage contract, gender, and nation is rewritten.

NOTES

1. See https://www.irishtimes.com/news/world/middle-east/israel-approves-controversial-jewish-nationality-law-1.3570017.

2. See the follow up discussion on Tedx https://www.youtube.com/watch?v=4-Fr3DqgXF0, December 2018.

3. https://www.lau.edu.lb/news-events/news/archive/we_need_a_civil_personal_law_t/.

4. See the following newspaper article: https://www.theguardian.com/society/2016/feb/25/italy-passes-watered-down-bill-recognising-same-sex-civil-unions. While the law primarily enabled same-sex couples to marry, it also allowed all couples, irrespective of their genders, to marry under civil law, not ecclesiastical law, hence the Catholic Church opposed it.

5. See https://www.cfr.org/backgrounder/same-sex-marriage-global-comparisons. Only Israel recognizes same-sex unions performed overseas. Australia recognized same sex marriage in 2017.

6. Interreligious marriages require a conversion between religions for a marriage to take place.

Glossary of Arabic Terms

Ahlin	Religious subjects or community
Alawites	Religious sect within Shi'ite Islam
'Almani	Secular
Ard	Land
Ba'ina	Dowry
Bayt	Patrilineage
Bint 'amm	Paternal uncle's daughter
Day'aa	Village
Dhimmis	Non-Muslim subjects under protection of Islamic law who were people of the book including Jews, Christians and sometimes Zoroastrians and Hindus.
Druze	Minority religious sect in Lebanon
Emir	Prince or commander
Fiqh	Islamic jurisprudence
Hadith	Teachings and sayings of the Prophet
Hanafi	Sunni school of Islamic law (one of four)
Hanbali	Sunni school of Islamic law (one of four)
Hijaz	The holy land of Islam, including Mecca and Medina in Saudi Arabia
'Idda	Waiting period
Ijma	Consensus of legal reasoning
Iqta	System of feudal property relations and tax farming in Islamic empires
Isma	Clause in marriage contract
Ismailis	Religious sect within Shi'ite Islam
Ja'fari	Shi'ite school of Islamic law (one of two main schools)
Jizya	Poll tax paid by non-Muslims under Islamic law

Khul	Female-initiated divorce
Maghrib	The North African region
Maher	Bride price
Mahsoubieh	Kinship capital derived from an extended family network
Malaki	Sunni school of Islamic law (one of four)
Millet	Non-Muslim religious community within the Ottoman Empire with their own autonomous personal status law. It is debatable as to whether the term *millet* also referred to Muslim communities, as Islam was the religion of state.
Moudawana	Morocco's family law code
Muqata'jis	Feudal landlord
Mutasarrif	Governor
Mutasarrifate	Semiautonomous region within the Ottoman Empire in present-day Lebanon
Mutayer	Landless serf
Muwatinin	Citizens
Niqa	Islamic marriage contract
Pasha	Governor
Qadi	Judge of Islamic Law
Qiyas	Foundation of Islamic legal reasoning
Qur'an	Islamic holy book and revelation of God
Shafi'i	Sunni school of Islamic law (one of four)
Shari'a	Islamic holy law
Sheikh	Muslim spiritual leader
Shi'ite	Second largest branch of Islam
Shura	Consultation
Sunna	Deeds and pronouncements of the Prophet.
Sunni	Largest branch of Islam
Ta'ifa	Sect
Talaq al-tafwid	Women's delegated right to divorce
Talaq	Islamic divorce
Talaq-e-biddat	Instant Divorce (repudiation)
Ulama	Islamic scholars and leaders
Wahhabism	Religious doctrine and religious movement founded by Muhammad ibn Abd al-Wahhab
Wali	Legal guardian
Walayah	Male guardianship system
Zaidi	Shiite school of Islamic law (one of two main schools)
Zina	Sexual transgression outside of marriage

Bibliography

Abi Yaghi, Marie-Noelle, Myriam Catusse, and Mriam Younes. 2017. "From isqat an-nizam at-ta'ifi to the Garbage Crisis Movement: Political Identities and Antisectarian Movements." In *Lebanon Facing the Arab Uprisings: Constraints and Adaptation*, edited by R. Di Peri and D. Meier, 73–91. London: Palgrave Macmillan.

Abu-Lughod, Lila. 2013. *Do Muslim Women Need Saving*. Harvard: Harvard University Press.

Ahmed, Fatuma A, and Hannah M. Macharia. 2013. "Women, Youth and the Egyptian Arab Spring." *Peace Review: A Journal of Social Justice* 25:359–366.

Ahmed, Leila. 1992. *Women and Gender in Islam: Historical Roots of a Modern Debate*. New Haven: Yale University Press.

Al-Ali, Nadje. 2000. *Secularism, Gender and the State in the Middle East: The Egyptian Women's Movement, Cambridge Middle East Studies*. Cambridge: Cambridge University Press.

Al-Ali, Nadje. 2012. "Gendering the Arab Spring." *Middle East Journal of Culture and Communication* 5:26–31.

Al-Amin, E. 2009. "What Really Happened in the Lebanese Elections?" *Counterpunch Weekend Edition* (June 12–14). Accessed June 16, 2009. doi:http://www.counterpunch.org/amin06122009.html.

Al-Rasheed, Madawi. 2013. *A Most Masculine State: Gender, Politics and Religion in Saudi Arabia*. Cambridge: Cambridge University Press.

Alonso, Andoni, and Pedro J. Oiarzabal. 2010. *Diasporas in the New Media Age: Identity, Politics, and Community*. Reno: University of Nevada Press.

Arenfeldt, Purnille, and Nawar Al-Hassan Golley. 2012. "Arab Women's Movements: Developments, Priorities, and Challenges." In *Mapping Arab Women's Movements: A Century of Transformation from Within*, edited by Purnille Arenfeldt and Nawar Al-Hassan Golley, 1–7. Cairo: The American University in Cairo Press.

Asad, Talal. 2003. *Formations of the Secular: Christianity, Islam, Modernity*. Stanford: Stanford University Press.

Assaf, Georges. 2009. "Reform from the Bottom: How the Judiciary and Civil Society Can Lessen the Sectarian Grip on Lebanese Citizens." *Daily Star*, October 1.

Awan, Akil N., Andrew Hoskins, and Ben O'Loughlin. 2011. *Radicalisation and Media: Connectivity and Terrorism in the New Media Ecology, Media, War and Security*. Abingdon; New York: Routledge.

Azar, Sahar, and Safa Azar. 2016. "Waste Related Pollutions and Their Potential Effect on Cancer Incidences in Lebanon." *Journal of Environmental Protection* 7:778–783.

Aziz, Jean. 2013. *Lebanon's First Civil Marriage A Sign of Change. Al Monitor*. April 28. https://www.al-monitor.com/pulse/originals/2013/04/lebanon-first-civil-marriage-political-change.html#ixzz67IdJ6gD1.

Babst, Gordon A., and Nicole M. Tellier. 2012. "One State of Two in Israel/Palestine: The Stress on Gender and Citizenship." *Arab Studies Quarterly* 34 (2):70–91.

Badran, M., and M. Cooke, eds. 1990. *Opening the Gates*. Bloomington: Indiana University Press.

Badran, Margot. 2005. "Between Secular and Islamic Feminism/s: Reflections on the Middle East and Beyond." *Journal of Middle East Women's Studies* 1 (1):6–28.

Badran, Margot. 2009. "Islamic Feminism: What's in a Name." In *Feminism in Islam: Secular and Religious Convergences*, edited by Margot Badran, 242–253. Oxford: Oneworld Press.

Barkawi, Tarak. 2011. "The Globalisation of Revolution." *Al Jazeera*. http://www.aljazeera.com/indepth/opinion/2011/03/2011320131934568573.html.

Barrington, Lisa. 2016. "Export Solution to Lebanon's Trash Crisis Scrapped." *Reuters*, February 20, 2016. https://www.reuters.com/article/us-lebanon-rubbish/export-solution-to-lebanons-trash-crisis-scrapped-idUSKCN0VS1OF.

Batrouney, Trevor. 1992. "The Lebanese in Australia 1880–1989." In *The Lebanese in the World: A Century of Emigration*, edited by Albert Hourani and Nadim Shehadi, 413–422. London: The Centre for Lebanese Studies & I.B Tauris.

Batrouney, Trevor, and Andrew Batrouney. 1985. *The Lebanese in Australia*. Melbourne: Ae Press.

Beinin, Joel, and Frederic Vairel. 2013. "Introduction." In *The Middle East and North Africa: Beyond Classical Social Movement Theory*, edited by Joel Beinin and Frederic Vairel. Stanford, CA: Stanford University Press.

Berg, Bruce. 2009. *Qualitative Research Methods for the Social Sciences*. Boston: Allyn and Bacon. Reprint, Seventh.

Bourdieu, Pierre. 1998. *Masculine Domination*. Stanford: Standford University Press.

Bryman, Alan, and Emma Bell. 2011. *Business Research Methods*. Oxford: Oxford University Press.

Buckingham, David, and Rebekah Willett. 2006. *Digital Generations: Children, Young People, and the New Media*. Mahwah, NJ: Lawrence Erlbaum Associates.

Charafeddine, Fahima. 2009. *Predicament of Lebanese Women Married to Non-Lebanese: Field Analytical Study*. Beirut: United Nations Development Program/ Lebanese Women's Rights and Nationality Law Project.

Charrad, Mounira. 2001. *States and Women's Rights: The Making of Postcolonial Tunisia, Algeria and Morocco*. Berkeley: University of California Press.

Charrad, Mounira. 2011a. "Gender in the Middle East: Islam, State, Agency." *The Annual Review of Sociology* 37:417–437.

Charrad, Mounira. 2011b. "Central and Local Patrimonialism: State-Building in Kin-Based Societies." *Annals, AAPSS*, July: 49–68.

Chester, Jeff. 2007. *Digital Destiny: New Media and the Future of Democracy*. New York: New Press, Distributed by W.W. Norton.

Chung, Fay, and Preben Kaarsholm. 2006. *Re-living the Second Chimurenga: Memories from the Liberation Struggle in Zimbabwe*. Uppsala Harare, Zimbabwe: Nordic Africa Institute; Weaver Press.

Cleaver, Tessa, and Marion Wallace. 1990. *Namibia, Women in War*. London: Zed.

Cobban, Helena. 1985. *The Making of Modern Lebanon*. London: Hutchinson.

Coleman, Isobel. 2013. *Paradise Beneath Her Feet: How Women Are Transforming the Middle East*. New York: Random House.

Cooke, Miriam. 1994–1995. "Arab Women Arab Wars." *Cultural Critique* 29 (Winter):5–29.

Cooke, Miriam. 1988. *War's Other Voices: Women Writers on the Lebanese Civil War*. Cambridge: Cambridge University Press.

Cooke, Miriam. 2016. "Women and the Arab Spring: A Transnational, Feminist Revolution." In *Women's Movements in Post-"Arab Spring" North Africa. Comparative Feminist Studies*, edited by F Sadiqi. New York: Palgrave Macmillan.

Covell, Andy. 2000. *Digital Convergence: How the Merging of Computers, Communications, and Multimedia Transforming Our Lives*. Newport, RI: Aegis Publishing Group.

CRTD.A/UNDP. 2004. *CRTD.A "Gender, Citizenship and Nationality Programme," Denial of Nationality: The Case of Arab Women*. Beirut: CRTD.A and UNDP POGAR.

Cuno, Kenneth M. 2015. *Modernizing Marriage: Family, Ideology, and Law in Nineteenth- and Early Twentieth Century Egypt*. Syracuse: Syracuse University Press.

Dabashi, Hamid. 2012. *The Arab Spring: The End of Postcolonialism*. London and New York: Zed Books.

Dahelrup, Drude. 2009. "Women in Arab Parliaments: Can Gender Quotas Contribute to Democratization?" *Al-Raida*, Summer/Fall (126–127):28–38.

Dakroub, Hussein. 2017. "Aoun Issues Stern Warning Against 1960 Law, Extension." *Daily Star*. April 21, accessed December 2019. http://www.dailystar.com.lb/News/Lebanon-News/2017/Apr-21/402739-aoun-issues-stern-warning-against-1960-law-extension.ashx.

Deeb, Sarah El. 2018. "Lebanon Pushes for More Women in Politics." *The Daily Star Lebanon*, January 22.

Dobbelaere, Karel. 1999. "Towards an Integrated Perspective of the Processes Related to the Descriptive Concept of Secularization." *Sociology of Religion* 60 (3):229–247.

Donk, Wim B. H. J. van de. 2004. *Cyberprotest: New Media, Citizens, and Social Movements*. London, New York: Routledge.

Dorigo, Linda. 2013. "Women Under Seige: Stateless in Lebanon." The Arab Studies Institute, Last Modified April 3, accessed June 17. http://photography.jadaliyya.com/pages/index/11000/women-under-seige_stateless-in-lebanon.

Doron, Assa. 2012. " Mobile Persons: Cell Phones, Gender and the Self in North India." *The Australian Pacific Journal of Anthropology* 13 (5):414–433. doi: 10.1080/14442213.2012.726253.

Doron, Assa, and Robin Jeffrey. 2018. *Waste of a Nation: Garbage and Growth in India*. Cambridge: Harvard University Press.

Economist. 2016. "Census and Sensibility, Lebanon." *Economist* 421 (9014):39–40.

El-Cheikh, Nadia M. 1998. "The 1998 Proposed Civil Marriage Law in Lebanon: The Reactionof the Muslim Communities." *Yearbook of Islamic and Middle Eastern Law Online* 5:147–161.

El-Helou, Marguerite. 2009. "Women Quota in Parliament: A False Promise?" *Al-Raida*, Summer/Fall (126–127).

El-Makari, Mark. 2009. "The Proposed Gender Quota in Lebanon: Legal Crisis or Democratic Transformation?" *Al-Raida*, Summer/Fall (126–127):39–51.

Eltahawy, Mona. 2015. *Headscarves and Hymens: Why the Middle East Needs a Sexual Revolution*. New York: Farrar, Straus and Giroux.

Engels, Frederick. 1902. *The Origin of the Family, Private Property and the State*. Vol. 1st English language edition. Chicago: Charles H. Kerr & Co.

Farha, Mark. 2012. "Global Gradations of Secularism. The Consociational, Communal and Coercive Paradigms." *Comparative Sociology* (11):354–386.

Fawaz, Alia. 2018. "Environmentalist, Activist, Engineer, Visionary: The Many Hats of Ziad Abi Chaker." *Home: The Soul of Lebanon* (7). https://mylebanonmyhome.com/environmentalist-activist-engineer-ziad-abi-chaker/.

Fisher, Karen. 2009. "Social Media Versus Social Technology: Refining Definitions." *Web 2.0 Blog*. http://www.web20blog.org/2009/01/04/social-media-vs-social-technology/.

Fisher Onar, Nora, and Hande Paker. 2012. "Towards Cosmopolitan Citizenship? Women's Rights in Divided Turkey." *Theory and Society: Renewal and Critique of Social Theory*, May 24.

Fisk, Robert. 2002. *Pity the Nation: The Abduction of Lebanon*. New York: Nation Books.

Flew, Terry. 2008. *New Media: An Introduction*. 3rd ed. South Melbourne, VIC: Oxford University Press.

Foblets, Marie-Claire. 2016. "New Family Law Codes in Middle Eastern Countries: Reforms that Are Faithful to Islamic Tradition?" In *Changing God's Law: The Dynamics of Middle Eastern Family Law*, edited by N. Yassari, 1–14. New York: Routledge.

Fowler, Bridget. 2003. "Reading Pierre Bourdieu's Masculine Domination: Notes Towards An Intersectional Analysis of Gender, Culture and Class." *Cultural Studies* 17 (3–4):468–494.

Freeman, Jo. 2009. "The Women's Movement." In *The Social Movements Reader: Cases and Concepts*, edited by Jeff Goodwin and James M. Jasper, 15–24. Oxford: Wiley-Blackwell.

Galer, Sophia Smith. 2018. "Lebanon Is Drowning in its Own Waste." *BBC*, March 28, 2018. http://www.bbc.com/future/story/20180328-lebanon-is-drowning-in-its-own-waste.

Garrison, Marsha. 1983. "Marriage: The Status of Contract." *University of Pennsylvania Law Review* 131 (4):1039–1062. doi: 10.2307/3311990.

Geagea, Nayla, Layal Mroue, and Georgina Manok. 2014. *Personal Status in Lebanon: Current Legislative Framework and the Proposed Recommendations*. Beirut: Lebanese Economic Association.

Ghabour, Ibrhaim. 2010–2017. *Introduction to Syrian Personal Status and Family Law*. Jura Law, Teller Books.

Ghaddar, Sima. 2017. *Second-Class Citizenship: Lebanese Women Fight to Pass Nationality to Children and Spouses*. New York: The Century Foundation.

Giddens, Anthony. 1991. *Modernity and Self-identity: Self and Society in the Late Modern Age*. Stanford: Stanford University Press.

Giddens, Anthony. 1992. *The Transformation of Intimacy: Sexuality, Love and Eroticism in Modern Societies*. Cambridge: Polity Press.

Goodman, David. 2011. "In British Riots, Social Media and Face Masks Are the Focus." *New York Times*, accessed November 17. http://thelede.blogs.nytimes.com/2011/08/11/social-media-and-facemasks-are-targets-after-british-riots/.

Gregory, Chris A. 1982. *Gifts and Commodities*. Edited by John Eatwell, *Studies in Political Economy*. London: Academic Press.

Gulick, John. 1954. "Conservatism and Change in a Lebanese Village." *Middle East Journal* 9:295–305.

Hage, Ghassan. 1989. "The Fetishism of Identity: Class, Politics and Processes of Identification in Lebanon." PhD, Political Science, Macquarie University.

Hage, Ghassan. 2001. "The Condition of Lebanon Since 1958." In *The Australian People: An Encyclopedia of the Nation, its People and Their Origins*, edited by James Jupp, 559–561. Cambridge: Cambridge University Press.

Hage, Ghassan. 2004. "Identity Fetishism: Capitalism and White Self-Racialization." In *Racialization: Studies in Theory and Practice*, edited by Karim Murji. Oxford: Oxford University Press.

Hanf, Theodor. 2015. *Co-Existence in War Time Lebanon: Decline of a State and Rise of a Nation*. 2nd ed. London: I.B Taurus.

Hermez, Sami. 2011. "Activism as 'Part-Time' Activity: Searching for Commitment and Solidarity in Lebanon." *Cultural Dynamics* 23 (1):41–55. https://doi.org/10.1177/0921374011403353.

Hirst, Martin, and John Harrison. 2007. *Communication and New Media: From Broadcast to Narrowcast*. Oxford: Oxford University Press.

Hitti, Philip, K. 1965. *A Short History of Lebanon*. London: Macmillan.

Hourani, Albert. 1991. *A History of the Arab Peoples*. London: Faber and Faber.

Howard, Philip N., and M.M. Hussain. 2013. *Democracy's Fourth Wave? Digital Media and the Arab Spring*. Oxford: Oxford University Press.

Human Rights Watch. 2014. *Lebanon: Domestic Violence Law Good, But Incomplete*. Online: Human Rights Watch. https://www.hrw.org/news/2014/04/03/lebanon-domestic-violence-law-good-incomplete.

Human Rights Watch. 2015. *Unequal and Unprotected: Women's Rights under Lebanese Personal Status Laws*. London and Washington, DC: Human Rights Watch.

Human Rights Watch. 2016. *Boxed In: Women and Saudi Arabia Male Guardianship System*. Washington, DC: Human Rights Watch.

Human Rights Watch. 2017. *"As If You're Inhaling Your Death": The Health Risks of Burning Waste in Lebanon*. Online: Human Rights Watch.

Humphrey, Michael. 1989. "Religion, Law and Family Disputes in a Lebanese Muslim Community in Sydney." In *Ethnicity, Class and Gender*, edited by Marie de Lepervanche and Gillian Bottomley. Sydney: Allen and Unwin.

Humphrey, Michael. 1998. *Islam, Multiculturalism and Transnationalism: From the Lebanese Diaspora*. London, New York: The Centre for Lebanese Studies in association with I.B Tauris Publishers.

Humphrey, Michael. 2011. "The Special Tribunal for Lebanon: Emergency Law, Trauma and Justice." *Arab Studies Quarterly* (Spring):1–27.

Hussein, Shakira. 2016. *From Victims to Suspects: Muslim Women Since 9/11*. Sydney: New South Books.

Hyndman-Rizk, Nelia. 2015. "Forbidden Love in Lebanon: Reflections on the Civil Marriage Debate." In *In Line With the Divine: The Struggle For Women's Rights in Lebanon*, edited by Guita Hourani, Rita Stephan and Cornelia Horn, 89–102. Berlin and Washington, DC: Abelian Academic.

IECCEC (Islam in Europe Committee of the Conference of European Churches). 2000. "Marriages Between Christians and Muslims: Pastoral Guidelines for Christians and Churches in Europe." *Journal of Muslim Minority Affairs* 20 (1):147–160. doi: https://doi.org/10.1080/13602000050008960.

IPU. 2019. *Women in National Parliaments*. Inter Parliamentary Union. 1 February. http://archive.ipu.org/wmn-e/classif.htm.

Jankowiak, Walter, and Thomas Paladino. 2008. "Desiring Sex, Longing for Love: A Tripartite Conundrum." In *Intimacies: Love and Sex Across Cultures*, edited by W Jankowiak, 1–37. New York: Columbia University Press.

Jay, Martin, and Ruby Russell. 2017. "Lebanon Garbage Crisis Pollutes Mediterranean." *DW.Com*, June 14, 2017. https://www.dw.com/en/lebanon-drowning-in-rubbish/av-47147917.

Jenkins, Henry. 2008. *Convergence Culture: Where Old and New Media Collide*. New York: New York University Press.

Joseph, Suad. 1999a. "Brother-Sister Relationships: Connectivity, Love and Power in the Reproduction of Patriarchy in Lebanon." In *Intimate Selving in Arab Families*, edited by Suad Joseph, 113–141. Syracuse, NY: Syracuse University Press.

Joseph, Suad. 1999b. "My Son/Myself, My Mother/Myself: Paradoxical Relationalities of Patriarchal Connectivity." In *Intimate Selving in Arab Families: Gender, Self and Identity*, edited by S. Joseph, 174–191. New York: Syracuse University Press.

Joseph, Suad. 1996. "Gender and Citizenship in Middle Eastern States." *Middle East Report* 198 (26):4–11.

Joseph, Suad. 2000. "Civil Myths, Citizenship, and Gender in Lebanon." In *Gender and Citizenship in the Middle East*, edited by Suad Joseph, 107–137. New York: Syracuse University Press.

Joseph, Suad. 2010. "Gender and Citizenship in the Arab World." *Al-Raida*, Spring/Summer (129–130):8–18.

KAFA. 2019. "Personal Status." KAFA, accessed March 14. https://www.kafa.org.lb/en/node/87.

Kandiyoti, Deniz. 1988. "Bargaining with Patriarchy." *Gender & Society* 2 (3):274–290.

Keddie, Nikki R. 2006. *Women in the Middle East: Past and Present*. Princeton and Oxford: Princeton University Press.

Kepler-Lewis, Ralph. 1968. "Hadchite; A Study of Emigration in A Lebanese Village." PhD, Faculty of Political Science, Columbia University.

Khalil, Joe. 2017. "Lebanon's Waste Crisis: An Exercise of Participation Rights." *New Media & Society* 19 (5):701–712.

Khamis, Sahar, and Amel Mili. 2017. "Introductory Themes." In *Arab Women's Activism and Socio-Political Transformation: Unfished Gendered Revolutions*, edited by Sahar Khamis and Amel Mili, 1–23. Cham, Switzerland: Palgrave Macmillan.

Khraiche, Dana. 2012. "Women's Spring: Is Lebanon Ready for a Feminist Political Party?" *The Daily Star Lebanon*, February 24.

Kodeih, Naji, Jim Puckett, and Kuepouo. 2016. "Press Release: Lebanon Plans to Dump Its Garbage on Africa or Middle East Neighbors." *IPEN: A Toxics Free Future*, accessed February 4, https://ipen.org/news/press-release-lebanon-plans-dump-its-garbage-africa-or-middle-east-neighbors.

Kohn, Alice. 2016. "Trash Crisis Forces Lebanon's Environmental Awakening." DW.Com. https://p.dw.com/p/2UGPD.

Korotayev, Andrey V., Leonid M. Issaev, Sergey Yu. Malkov, and Alisa R. Shishkina. 2014. "The Arab Spring: A Quantitative Analysis." *Arab Studies Quarterly* 36 (2):149–169. doi:10.13169/arabstudquar.36.2.0149.

Kottak, Conrad. P. 1994. *Cultural Anthropology*. 6th ed. New York: McGraw Hill, INC. Original edition, 1974. Reprint, Sixth.

Kraidy, Marwan. 2016. "Trashing the Sectarian System? Lebanon's 'You Stink' Movement and the Making of Affective Publics." *Communication and the Public* 1 (1):19–26.

Krook, Mona Lena. 2009. "Gender Quotas in Parliament." *Al-Raida,* Summer/Fall (126–127):8–18.

Lerner, Gerda. 1986. *The Creation of Patriarchy*. Oxford: Oxford University Press.

Levi-Strauss, Claude. 1949. *The Elementary Structures of Kinship*. Oxford: Alden and Mowbray.

Levi-Strauss, Claude. 2000 (1963). "Structural Analysis in Linguistics and Anthropology." In *Anthropological Theory: An Introductory History*, edited by R. Jon McGee and Richard L. Warms, 332–347. Mountain View: Mayfield Publishing Company.

Lewis, Bernard. 1997. *The Middle East: A Brief History of the Last 2000 Years*. New York: Scribner.

Liddell, James. 2009. "Gender Quotas in Clientelist Systems: The Case of Morocco's National List." *Al-Raida,* Summer/Fall (126–127):79–88.

Lyons, Tanya. 2004. *Guns and Guerilla Girls: Women in the Zimbabwean National Liberation Struggle*. Trenton, NJ: Africa World Press.

Mahmood, Saba. 2005. *Politics of Piety: The Islamic Revival and the Feminist Subject*. Princeton: Princeton University Press.

Mahmood, Saba. 2016. *Religious Difference in a Secular Age: A Minority Report*. Princeton: Princeton University Press.

Majed, Rima. 2016. "In the Arab World, Sectarianism Is Real, Sects Are Not." *Al Jazeera*. www.aljazeera.com.

Maroun, Bechara. 2013. "Place des Martyrs, 'yes' to Civil Marriage." Last Modified May 2, 2013. http://www.lorientlejour.com/category/%C3%80+La+Une/article/799399/Le_mariage_civil_a_l%27honneur%2C_hier_place_des_Martyrs.html.

Marx, Karl. 1967 (1867). *Capital*. Vol. One. New York: International Publishers Co., Inc.

Massena, Florence. 2016. "Lebanon Holds Breath for Deal to Export Trash Abroad." *Al-Monitor: The Pulse of the Middle East*, February 1, 2016. https://www.al-monit or.com/pulse/originals/2016/02/lebanon-trash-crisis-tender-export-waste.html.

Mauss, Marcel. 1967 (1925). *The Gift: Forms and Functions of Exchange in Archaic Societies*. New York: W. W. Norton.

McAdam, D., Tarrow, S., & Tilly, C. 2001. *Dynamics of Contention (Cambridge Studies in Contentious Politics)*. Cambridge: Cambridge University Press. doi:10.1017/CBO9780511805431.

McGee, R. Jon, and Richard L. Warms. 2000. "Structuralism." In *Anthropological Theory: An Introductory History*, edited by R. Jon McGee and Richard L. Warms, 330–332. Mountain View,: Mayfield Publishing Company.

McGuigan, Jim. 2007. "Technological Determinism and Mobile Privatization." In *New Media Worlds: Challenges for Convergence*, edited by Tim Dwyer Virginia Nightingale, 5–18. Melbourne: Oxford University Press.

Mernissi, Fatima. 1987. *Beyond The Veil: Male-Female Dynamics in Modern Muslim Society*. Revised ed. Bloomington and Indianapolis: Indiana University Press. Original edition, 1975. Reprint, 1987.

Mikdashi, Maya. 2010. "A Legal Guide to Being a Lebanese Woman Part 1." [Critical Essay]. Arab Studies Institute, Last Modified March 8, 2013. http://www.jada liyya.com/pages/index/376/a-legal-guide-to-being-a-lebanese-woman.

Mikdashi, Maya. 2014. "Sex and Sectarianism: The Legal Architecture of Lebanese Citizenship." *Comparative Studies of South Asia, Africa and the Middle East* 34 (2):279–293.

Mili, Amer. 2017. "Citizenship and Gender Equality in the Crade of the Arab Spring." In *Arab Women's Activism and Socio-Political Transformation: Unfinished Gender Revolutions*, edited by S. Khamis and A. Mili. Philadelphia University of Philadelphia Press.

Moghadam, Valentine. 2004. "Patriarchy in Transition: Women and the Changing Family in the Middle East." *Journal of Comparative Family Studies* 35 (2):137–162.

Moghadam, Valentine. 2009. "Women, Politics, and Gender Quotas." *Al-Raida*, Summer/Fall (126–127):18–27.

Moghadam, Valentine, and Farzaneh Roudi-Fahimi. 2005. *Reforming Family Laws to Promote Progress in the Middle East and North Africa*. Washington: PRB, Population Reference Bureau.

Mohanty, Chandra Talpade. 2011. "Foreward." In *Transnational Borderlands in Women's Global Networks*, edited by C. Roman-Odio and M. Sierra. London. Palgrave Macmillan.

Morsi, Rami, Rawn Safa, Serge Baroud, Chrine Fawaz, Jad Farha, Fadi El-Jardali, and Monique Chaaya. 2017. "The Protracted Waste Crisis and Physical Health of Workers in Beirut: A Comparative Cross-Sectional Study." *Environmental Health* 16 (39):1–6.

Moussawi, Fatima, and Nasser Yassin. 2017. *Dissecting Lebanese Law 293 On Domestic Violence: Are Women Protected?* Beirut: AUB Policy Institute.

Naber, Nadine, and Zeina Zaatari. March 2014. "Reframing the War on Terror: Feminist and Lesbian, Gay, Bisexual, Transgender, and Queer (LGBTQ) Activism in the Context of the 2006 Israeli Invasion of Lebanon." *Cultural Dynamics* 26 (1):91–111. doi: 10.1177/0921374013510803.

Nader, Laura. 2002. *The Life of the Law: Anthropological Projects*. Berkeley: University of California Press.

Naib, F. 2011. "Women of the Revolution: Egyptian Women Describe the Spirit of Tahrir and their Hope that the Equality they Found there Will Live On." [Online Newspaper]. *Al Jazeera*, Last Modified February 2011, accessed June 4. http://www.aljazeera.com/indepth/features/2011/02/2011217134411934738.html.

Najjar, Farah. 2018. "Why Women Are 'barely scratching the surface' of Lebanese Politics." *Al Jazeera*, May 6, 2018.

Nichols, Joel A. 2012a. *Marriage and Divorce in a Multicultural Context; Multi-Tiered Marriage and the Boundaries of Civil Law and Religion*. Cambridge University Press.

Nichols, Joel A. 2012b. "Multi-Tiered Marriage: Reconsidering the Boundaries of Civil Law and Religion." In *Marriage and Divorce in a Multicultural Context: Multi-Tiered Marriage and the Boundaries of Civil Law and Religion*, edited by Joel A. Nichols, 11–60. Cambridge, New York: Cambridge University Press.

Noueihed, Lin, and Alex Warren. 2012. *The Battle for the Arab Spring: Revolution, Counter-Revolution and the Making of a New Era*. New Haven: Yale University Press.

Ofeish, Sami A. 1999. "Lebanon's Second Republic: Secular Talk, Sectarian Application," *Arab Studies Quarterly* 21 (1):97–116.

O'Gorman, Eleanor. 2011. *The Front Line Runs through Every Woman: Women & Local Resistance in the Zimbabwean Liberation War, African Issues*. Woodbridge, Suffolk and Harare: James Currey Weaver Press.

Osseiran, Dala. 2018. "Women's Involvement in Politics Still Touchy Subject." *The Daily Star*. January 18, http://www.dailystar.com.lb/News/Lebanon-News/2018/Jan-18/434246-womens-involvement-in-politics-still-touchy-subject.ashx.

Pateman, Carole. 1988. *The Sexual Contract*. Cambridge: Polity.

Perry, Mark. 2011. "Ideas Kindle the Fire of Revolution, Not the Internet." *The Daily Star*. February 21, http://www.dailystar.com.lb/ArticlePrint.aspx?id=121325&mode=print.

Peteet, Julie Marie, and American Council of Learned Societies. 1991. *Gender in Crisis Women and the Palestinian Resistance Movement*. New York: Columbia University Press. https://gate.library.lse.ac.uk/idp/profile/Shibboleth/SSO?target=http://hdl.handle.net/2027/heb.04737&shire=https://quod.lib.umich.edu/Shibboleth.sso/SAML/POST&providerId=https://quod.lib.umich.edu/shibboleth-sp/acls.

Porta, Donatella Della, and Mario Diani. 2006. *Social Movements: An Introduction*. 2nd ed. Oxford: Blackwell.

Russell, Tom. 1985. "A Lebanon Primer." *MERIP Reports* 133 (June):17–19.

Sabat, Rita. 2012. "Translating Gender Equality Norms in Lebanon. Rita Sabat, Notre Dame University." Gender and Women's Studies in the Arab Region, American University of Shahjah, March 9.

Sadiki, Larbi. 2004. *The Search for Arab Democracy: Discourses and Counter-Discourses*. New York: Columbia University Press.

Sadiki, Larbi, and Youcef Bouandel. 2016. "The Post Arab Spring Reform: The Maghreb at a Cross Roads." *Digest of Middle East Studies* 25 (1):109–131.

Said, Edward. 1978. *Orientalism.* London: Penguin Books.

Sakr, Elias, and Nafez Qawas. 2009. "Intensive Lebanese Efforts Give Birth to Triumphant National-Unity Cabinet." *Daily Star*, November 10, 2009. http://www.dailystar.com.lb/article.asp?edition_id=1&categ_id=2&article_id=108525

Salibi, Kamal. 1971. "The Lebanese Identity." *Journal of Contemporary History* 6 (1, Nationalism and Separatism):76–86.

Salibi, Kamal. 1988. *A House of Many Mansions: The History of Lebanon Reconsidered.* London I.B Tauris and Co. Ltd.

Salisbury, Richard F. 1956. "Asymmetrical Marriage Systems." *American Anthropologist* 58 (4):639–655. doi: 10.1525/aa.1956.58.4.02a00050.

Seymour-Smith, Charlotte. 1986. *Palgrave Dictionary of Anthropology.* London: Macmillan Press.

Shehadeh, Lamia Rustum. 1998. "The Legal Status of Married Women in Lebanon." *International Journal of Middle East Studies* 30 (4):501–519.

Shehadeh, Lamia Rustum. 2010. "Gender-Relevant Legal Change in Lebanon." *Feminist Formations* 22 (3):210–228.

Sherman, Taylor, William Gould, and Sarah Ansari. 2014. "Introduction." In *From Subjects to Citizens: Society and Everday State in India and Pakistan, 1947–1970*, edited by Taylor Sherman, William Gould and Sarah Ansari. Delhi: Cambridge University Press.

Siham Yahya, Simon Boag, Anika Munshi, and Tal Litvak-Hirsch. 2016. "'Sadly, Not All Love Affairs Are Meant To Be . . .' Attitudes Towards Interfaith Relationships in a Conflict Zone." *Journal of Intercultural Studies* 37 (3):265–285.

Stephan, Rita. 2010. "Couple's Activism in Lebanon: The Legacy of Laure Moghaizel." *Women's Studies International Forum* 33 (2010):533–541.

Stephan, Rita. 2012a. "A Couples Activism for Women's Rights in Lebanon: The Legacy of Larue Moghaizel." Dissertation, University of Texas Austin.

Stephan, Rita. 2012b. "Women's Rights Activism in Lebanon." In *Mapping Arab Women's Movements: A Century of Transformations from Within*, edited by Purnille Arenfeldt and Nawar Al-Hassan Golley, 111–133. Cairo: American University of Cairo Press.

Stephan, Rita. 2014. Four Waves of Lebanese Feminism. *E-International Relations*, November 7. https://www.e-ir.info/2014/11/07/four-waves-of-lebanese-feminism/.

Stephan, Rita. 2017. "Lebanese Women's Rights Beyond the Cedar Revolution." In *Arab Women's Activism and Socio-Political Transformation: Unfinished Gendered Revolutions*, edited by Sahar Khamis and Amel Mili, 73–107. Cham, Switzerland: Palgrave Macmillan.

Stephan, Rita. November 2019. "Not-So-Secret Weapons: Lebanese Women's Rights Activists and Extended Family Networks." *Social Problems* 66 (4):609–625, https://doi.org/10.1093/socpro/spy025.

SWMENA. 2011. "Focus on Lebanon: Attitudes Towards Policy Change Topic Brief." In *The Status of Women in the Middle East and North Africa Project.* Washington: International Foundation (IFES) for Electoral Systems and The Institute for Women's Policy Research (IWPR).

Szmolka, Inmaculada. 2015. "Exclusionary and Non-Consensual Transitions Versus Inclusive and Consensual Democratizations: The Cases of Egypt and Tunisia." *Arab Studies Quarterly* 37 (1):73–95.

The Daily Star. 2013a. "Bride's Family Rejects Her Battle for Civil Marriage in Lebanon." *The Daily Star*, January 26. http://www.dailystar.com.lb/ArticlePrint .aspx?id=203803&mode=print.

The Daily Star. 2013b. "Mufti Stance Against Civil Marriage Unacceptable: Hariri." *The Daily Star*, accessed June 17. http://www.dailystar.com.lb/News/Local-N ews/2013/Jan-31/204542-muftis-stance-against-civil-marriage-unacceptable-.a shx#axzz2JasXM154.

The Daily Star. 2013c. "A New Lebanon." [Editorial]. *The Daily Star*, Last Modified January 21, 2013. http://www.dailystar.com.lb/Opinion/Editorial/2013/Jan-21/20 3064-a-new-lebanon.ashx#axzz2Jv5LOxpr.

The Daily Star. 2013d. "UNHCR Stresses Need to Offer Syrian Refugees Safe Harbor." *The Daily Star Lebanon*, October 19, 2013, Middle East. http://www.dail ystar.com.lb/News/Middle-East/2013/Oct-19/235073-unhcr-stresses-need-to-off er-syrian-refugees-safe-harbor.ashx#axzz2iQKApMSQ.

The Daily Star. 2013e. "Sectarian Shackles." *The Daily Star*, January 30.

The Daily Star. 2017. "International Support Group for Lebanon Urges Greater Efforts for New Vote Law." *The Daily Star*, April 18. http://www.dailystar.com. lb/News/Lebanon-News/2017/Apr-18/402306-international-support-group-for-leb anon-urges-greater-efforts-for-new-vote-law.ashx?utm_source=Magnet&utm_medi um=Recommended%20Articles%20widget&utm_campaign=Magnet%20tools.

Thompson, Elizabeth. 2013. *Justice Interrupted: The Struggle for Constitutional Government in the Middle East*. Harvard University Press.

Thompson, Elizabeth. 2000. *Colonial Citizens: Republican Rights, Paternal Privilege, and Gender in French Syria and Lebanon*. New York: Columbia University Press.

Tilley, Charles, and Lesley J. Wood. 2009. *Social Movements 1768–2008*. 2nd ed. Boulder, London: Paradigm Publishers.

Traboulsi, Fawwaz. 2012. *A History of Modern Lebanon*. 2nd ed. London: Pluto Press. Original edition, 2007.

Turner, Eric. 2013. "New Movements, Digital Revolution, and Social Movement Theory." *Peace Review* 25 (3):376–383. doi: 10.1080/10402659.2013.816562.

UN Women. "Beijing and Its Follow Up." United Nations. http://www.un.org/wo menwatch/daw/beijing/.

UN Women. 2009. "Convention for the Elimination of All Forms Discrimination against Women." Original 1979. https://undocs.org/en/A/RES/34/180

UNDP. 2018a. *2018 Lebanese Parliamentary Elections: Results and Figures*. Online: United Nations Development Program (UNDP).

UNDP. 2018b. *Lebanon Gender Justice and the Law*. New York: UNDP, UN Women and UNFP.

UNDP. 2019. *Gender Development Index GDI*. United Nations Development Program.

UNESCO. 2019. *Education and Literacy, Lebanon*. http://uis.unesco.org/country/LB.

UNFPA. 2015. *Lebanon: Scorecard on Gender-based Violence*. UNFPA.

UNICEF. 2006. *Lebanon: MENA Gender Equality Profile, Status of Girls and Women in the Middle East and North Africa*. United Nations Children's Fund.

Wedeman, Ben. 2018. "Lebanon's Garbage Crisis Washes Up On the Beach." *CNN*. https://edition.cnn.com/2018/01/25/middleeast/lebanon-beach-garbage-crisis-intl/index.html.

Weiss, Max. 2010. *In the Shadow of Sectarianism: Law, Shi'ism and the Making of Modern Lebanon*. Cambridge: Harvard University Press.

Williams, Herbert. 1958. "Some Aspects of Culture and Personality in a Lebanese Maronite Village." PhD, Anthropology, University of Pennsylvania.

Wolf, Naomi. 2011. "The Middle East Feminist Revolution: Women Are Not Merely Joining Protests to Topple Dictators, they Are at the Centre of Demanding Social Change." *Al Jazeera*, Last Modified March 2011, accessed June 4. http://www.alja zeera.com/indepth/opinion/2011/03/201134111445686926.html.

World Bank 2013. *Opening the Doors: Gender Equality and Development in the Middle East and North Africa*. https://doi.org/10.1596/978-0-8213-9763-3.

World Bank. 2017. *Proportion of Seats Held by Women in National Parliaments*. World Bank Group.

World Bank. 2019. "Labour Force Participation Rate, Female: Selected Countries." https://data.worldbank.org/indicator/SL.TLF.CACT.FE.ZS?end=2016&locati ons=1A&start=1990&view.

Wright, Moira. 1984. "Marriage: From Status to Contract?" *Anglo-American Law Review* 13 (1):17–31. https://doi.org/10.1177/147377958401300102.

Zalzal, Marie Rose. 1997. "Secularism and Personal Status Codes in Lebanon: Interview with Marie Rose Zalzal, Esquire." *Middle East Report* 203 (Lebanon and Syria):37–39.

Zoglin, Kate. 2009. "Morocco's Family Code: Improving Equality for Women." *Human Rights Quarterly* 31 (4):964–984.

Index

About the Author

Dr Nelia Hyndman-Rizk was awarded a PhD in anthropology from the Australian National University in 2010. Her interdisciplinary research interests include migration and pilgrimage studies, the Lebanese diaspora, cultural diversity in organizations, women's rights movements in the Middle East, and gender and development. She has published widely, including in the *Journal of Middle East Women's Studies*, *Journal of Intercultural Studies*, *Gender and Education*, *Mashriq & Mahjar*, *Numen*, and *Anthropological Forum*. She is the author of two other books: *My Mother's Table: At Home in the Maronite Diaspora* (2011) and *Pilgrimage in the Age of Globalization: Constructions of the Sacred and Secular in Late Modernity* (2012). She is a lecturer in "Cross Cultural Management" in the School of Business at the University of New South Wales, Canberra.

Contact: n.hyndman-rizk@unsw.edu.au

www.ingramcontent.com/pod-product-compliance
Lightning Source LLC
Chambersburg PA
CBHW050610280326
41932CB00016B/2984